THE SENATE AND TREATIES
1789–1817

THE SENATE AND TREATIES

1789–1817

THE DEVELOPMENT OF THE TREATY-MAKING FUNCTIONS OF THE UNITED STATES SENATE DURING THEIR FORMATIVE PERIOD

BY

RALSTON HAYDEN

DA CAPO PRESS • NEW YORK • 1970

A Da Capo Press Reprint Edition

This Da Capo Press edition of
The Senate and Treaties, 1789-1817,
is an unabridged republication of the
first edition published in New York in 1920.

Library of Congress Catalog Card Number 73-127295

SBN 306-71164-8

Copyright, 1920 by the University of Michigan

Published by Da Capo Press
A Division of Plenum Publishing Corporation
227 West 17th Street, New York, N.Y. 10011

THE SENATE AND TREATIES
1789–1817

THE SENATE AND TREATIES

1789–1817

THE DEVELOPMENT OF THE TREATY-MAKING FUNCTIONS OF THE UNITED STATES SENATE DURING THEIR FORMATIVE PERIOD

BY

RALSTON HAYDEN, Ph.D.

ASSISTANT PROFESSOR OF POLITICAL SCIENCE
UNIVERSITY OF MICHIGAN

New York

THE MACMILLAN COMPANY

London: Macmillan & Company, Limited

1920

All rights reserved

THE·PLIMPTON·PRESS
NORWOOD·MASS·U·S·A

TO
MY MOTHER AND FATHER

PREFACE

THIS book is a study in detail of the treaty-making powers of the United States Senate during the formative period of their history. This period is conceived to extend from 1789 to just a little beyond the first twenty-five years of government under the Constitution. No powers of the federal government underwent a more interesting development during this first quarter-century than did those which have to do with the making of treaties. There are good reasons for this. The treaty clause of the Constitution is so flexible that the exact relations of the Senate and the executive in treaty-making could be worked out only in actual practice. And there never has been a period in the history of this nation when foreign relations — threats of war, avoidances of armed conflicts, diplomatic defeats and victories, treaties made and denounced — have played so vital a part in the affairs of the government and in the lives of the people. The young republic was fixing her status in the family of nations — finding her level among a jostling throng who regarded her with indifferent, hostile, or designing eyes. Consequently that part of her constitutional organization which concerned treaty-making, and foreign relations generally, was rapidly developed by constant application to the problems of actual government.

ix

After the War of 1812 the United States turned
her thoughts and her energies more largely into
domestic channels. Her treaty-making power was
exercised in a new spirit after 1815. But if the
spirit of American diplomacy has changed with the
generations since Monroe entered the White House,
the manner in which this country has made the international agreements which are also her national
laws has been altered but little. This is particularly
true of the manner in which the Senate has performed its part in the making of treaties. The
Senate is a conservative body. Its procedure in
dealing with treaties and its relations with the executive in the performance of their joint functions
are to-day very much as they were a century ago,
although quite different from what they were expected to be in 1789. It is for these reasons that
the first twenty-five years under the Constitution
have been said to be the formative period in the
history of the treaty-making functions of the
Senate.

In the events of these years the writer has attempted to discover the conception of the place of
the Senate in treaty-making then held by the
various departments of the government, to trace
the development of the procedure of the Senate in
the transaction of treaty business, to ascertain the
relations between the Senate and the executive in
this field, and to investigate the effect of the position of the Senate in our constitutional system upon
the relations between the United States and other
nations. The study has been carried to the year
1817 for the purpose of examining the early exercise

of the treaty functions after they had reached their normal development.

The writer makes grateful acknowledgment of his obligations to Professor Jesse S. Reeves, under whose direction the work was undertaken and completed, to Professor Ulrich B. Phillips for carefully reading the text, and to his wife for valuable literary assistance. He is also indebted to *The American Journal of International Law* for permission to reprint as Chapter VIII an article which first appeared in that magazine.

RALSTON HAYDEN

ANN ARBOR, MICHIGAN
October, 1919

TABLE OF CONTENTS

CHAPTER I

CHAPTER II

THE
SENATE AND TREATIES

CHAPTER I

THE FIRST EXERCISE OF THE TREATY-MAKING POWER

On the twenty-fifth of May, 1789, while the Senate of the first Congress under the Constitution was engaged in debating the impost bill, a message was announced from the President of the United States to be delivered by General Knox. The distinguished messenger advanced, laid a bulky package of papers on the table before John Adams, the President of the Senate, and withdrew. The message transmitted to the upper house of the national legislature for its constitutional action two treaties with Indian tribes which had been negotiated and signed under the authority of the Continental Congress, together with sundry papers respecting them. It was ordered that the message of the President, with the accompanying papers, lie on the table for consideration, and the Senate returned to the debate in which it had been engaged.[1] Thus

---

[1] *Journal of the Executive Proceedings of the Senate of the United States of America. From the Commencement of the First to the Termination of the Nineteenth Congress* (Washington, 1828), I. 3. Cited below as *Sen. Exec. Jour.*

The Journal of William Maclay, United States Senator from Pennsylvania, 1789–1791, p. 49 (ed. 1890).

for the first time the Senate was faced with the executive duties laid upon it by the treaty clause of the Constitution. This clause declares, "He [the President] shall have power, by and with the advice and consent of the Senate, to make treaties, provided two-thirds of the Senators present concur; . . ." In these few words one of the most important powers of government is vested in the chief executive and the upper house of the Congress of the United States.[1] This bare grant told Washington and the members of the first Senate, as it tells us, merely that they were the joint possessors of this great power. With that elasticity in details which calls forth the admiration of the most discerning critic of our commonwealth, the Constitution left to successive Senates and to successive Presidents the problem and the privilege of determining under the stress of actual government the precise manner in which they were to make the treaties of the nation. At no subsequent period was more done to fix the relative powers of the President and the Senate in treaty-making, and to determine when and how the Senate should exercise its functions in this field than during the administrations of President Washington; the precedents which were then set, either on the basis of first-hand knowledge of the intention

[1] Burr, *The Treaty-Making Power of the United States and the Methods of Its Enforcement as Affecting the Police Powers of the States*, gives a clear account of the evolution of the treaty clauses of the Constitution in the Federal Convention. See also Moore, *International Law Digest*, V., xviii, for a discussion of the treaty power, the negotiation and conclusion of treaties, their ratification, agreements not submitted to the Senate, and the enforcement, interpretation, and termination of treaties.

of the framers of the Constitution, or through the necessities of the moment, have governed, in large part, the manner in which these functions have been performed ever since.

Certainly if any body of men ever have been qualified by experience to complete harmoniously in working detail the general plan of the constitutional convention of 1787, those men were the early Senators, the members of the early cabinets, and the first President. We have only to recall the personnel of these early governments to realize the extent to which this is true. Of the sixty-six men who served in the Senate during Washington's administrations, thirty-one had been members of the Continental Congress or of the Congress of the Confederation, twelve had helped draft the Constitution in the convention at Philadelphia, and ten had been members of state conventions which had ratified the federal instrument. Many had been active in organizing the rebellion and had served with distinction in the revolutionary forces and in the legislatures and constitutional conventions of their own states. Together with the members of the executive branch of the government they formed a body of men trained in politics and statesmanship, and eminently qualified to apply the newly made Constitution, not only wisely, but in the spirit of the great convention which had framed it, and of the state assemblies whose action had made it the supreme law of the land.

THE CONSULAR CONVENTION WITH FRANCE, 1788

Although the two pacts signed with Indian tribes at Fort Harmar and submitted to the Senate on May 2, 1789, were the first treaties to be laid before that body, it was to the ratification of a consular convention with France that the Senate first gave its advice and consent. This convention was a heritage from the government under the Confederation. Its previous history is succinctly told by J. C. B. Davis, as follows:

On the 25th of January, 1782, the Continental Congress passed an act authorizing and directing Dr. Franklin to conclude a Consular Convention with France on the basis of a scheme which was submitted to that body. Dr. Franklin concluded a very different convention, which Jay, the Secretary for Foreign Affairs, and Congress did not approve. Franklin having returned to America, the negotiations then fell upon Jefferson, who concluded the Convention of 1788.[1]

On June 11, 1789, Washington laid this convention before the Senate.[2] One of the striking aspects of the subsequent proceedings is the close relationship which was set up between the Senate and John Jay, who still filled the office of Secretary of Foreign Affairs, which had been held over from the government under the Confederation. The message submitting the convention, after briefly mentioning the

---

[1] Davis, "Notes Upon the Foreign Treaties of the United States," in *Treaties and Conventions Concluded Between the United States of America and Other Powers since July 4, 1776*, pp. 1217–1406. See pp. 1293–1295. Davis here gives a brief account of the negotiation of the treaty and the action of the Senate upon it.

[2] *Sen. Exec. Jour.*, I. 5.

purposes of the treaty and some of the circumstances
of its negotiation concluded:

> I now lay before you the original, by the hands of
> Mr. Jay, for your consideration and advice. The papers
> relative to this negotiation are in his custody, and he
> has my orders to communicate to you whatever official
> papers and information on the subject he may possess
> and you may require.

When received, the President's message was
simply read and ordered to lie for consideration.[1]
The Senate evidently desired to proceed in this new
business with the care and caution commensurate
with its importance, for on the following day the
message was again read before an order was adopted,
"That Mr. Jay furnish the Senate with an accurate
translation of the Consular Convention between His
Most Christian Majesty and the United States, and
a copy thereof for each member of the Senate." [2]
On the seventeenth the Senate sought further to
assure itself of the accuracy of this translation by
adopting an order that Jay examine it and report his
opinion of its fidelity. It also sought further information by asking the Secretary to lay before it all
the papers in his custody relative to the negotiation,
and whatever official papers and information on the
subject he might possess.[3] Four days later Jay was
requested "to attend the Senate to-morrow, at 12
o'clock, and to bring with him such papers as are
requisite to give full information, relative" to the
convention. Accordingly on the twenty-second the
Secretary "made the necessary explanations," after

---

[1] *Sen. Exec. Jour.*, I. 5.   [2] *Sen. Exec. Jour.*, I. 6.   [3] *Ibid.*

which he was asked to give his opinion as to how far
he conceived the faith of the United States to be engaged to ratify the convention in its existing "sense
or form." On the following Monday, this opinion
was presented in writing. Jay considered in detail
the circumstances in which the treaty had been
negotiated, and ended with the conclusion that it
should be ratified by the United States. Two days
later the Senate unanimously consented to the convention and advised the President to ratify it.[1]

This direct and personal intercourse between the
executive and the Senate is an indication of the
feeling which seems to have been prevalent that
the latter really was a council of advice upon treaties
and appointments — a council which expected to
discuss these matters directly with the other branch
of the government. There is much evidence to
support this view and also the conclusion that
the practice of personal consultation failed to become firmly established largely because it proved
to be an inconvenient and impracticable method of
transacting business. For its knowledge of treaties
the Senate came to depend, even during Washington's
administrations, upon documents submitted rather
than upon verbal reports. In the consideration of
the French consular convention both means were
used.

A second point of interest offered by this con-
vention is to be found in the motives which led the
Senate to advise and consent to its ratification.
On July 22, after Jay had personally explained the

[1] *Sen. Exec. Jour.*, I. 7, 8, 9; see Moore, *International Law Digest*, V. 587, for brief statement.

status of the convention, the Senate formally proposed this question to him:

Whereas a convention referred this day to the Senate, bears reference to a convention pending between the most Christian King and the United States, previous to the adoption of our present Constitution —

Resolved, That the Secretary of Foreign Affairs, under the former Congress, be requested to peruse the said Convention, and to give his opinion how far he conceives the faith of the United States to be engaged, either by former agreed stipulations, or negotiations entered into by our Minister at the Court of Versailles, to ratify, in its present sense or form, the Convention now referred to the Senate.[1]

In the written reply which he handed to the Senate five days later Jay recommended ratification. This recommendation seems to have been based upon two grounds: first, the general principle that a government was bound to ratify a treaty concluded by its minister acting in accordance with his instructions; second, that the Continental Congress had specifically promised to ratify this particular convention under certain conditions, which conditions had been met by France.

The report states that in the opinion of the Secretary:

There exist, in the convention of 1788, no variations from the original scheme sent to Dr. Franklin in 1782, nor from the convention of 1784, but such as render it less ineligible than either of the other two.

That, although he apprehends that this convention will prove more inconvenient than beneficial to the United States, yet he thinks that the circumstances under which it was formed render its being ratified by them indispensable.

[1] *Sen. Exec. Jour.*, I. 7.

The circumstances alluded to, are these:
The original scheme of 1782, however exceptionable, was framed and agreed to by Congress.

The convention of 1784 was modeled by that scheme, but in certain instances deviated from it; but both of them were to be perpetual in their duration.

On account of these deviations, Congress refused to ratify it, but promised to ratify one corresponding with the scheme, provided its duration was limited to eight or ten years; but they afterwards extended it to twelve.

Jay then cited a paragraph from the instructions sent to Jefferson in 1786, and quoted a letter accompanying them in which the Congress clearly recognized its obligation to ratify a treaty made in accordance with the scheme which, through their envoy, they had proposed to France. This recognition was in the following words:

" The original scheme of the convention is far from being unexceptionable, but a former Congress having agreed to it, it would be improper now to recede; and therefore Congress are content to ratify a convention made conformable to that scheme, and to their act of 25th January, 1782, provided a clause limiting its duration be added."

The report then continues:

On the 27th July, 1787, Congress gave to Mr. Jefferson a commission, in general terms, to negotiate and conclude with his most Christian Majesty, a convention for regulating the privileges, &c., of their respective Consuls.

In one of the letters then written him is this paragraph:

"Congress confide fully in your talents and discretion, and they will ratify any convention that is not liable to more objections than the one already, in part concluded, provided that an article, limiting its duration to a term not exceeding twelve years be inserted."

As the convention in question is free from several objections to which the one of 1784 was liable, and is, in every respect, preferable to it, and as it contains a clause limiting its duration to twelve years, it seems to follow, as of necessary consequence, that the United States ought to ratify it.[1]

Considering this transaction from beginning to end, it seems evident that from the time the Continental Congress of 1782 gave its assent to a plan for a convention, which its agent was to negotiate with France, until the final act of ratification in 1789 the government of the United States had acted in accordance with the principle of international law, that except under extraordinary circumstances a nation was bound to ratify any agreement which it had instructed its representative to make.[2] That the Congress of the Confederation felt the weight of this obligation is conclusively demonstrated by its instructions and letters to Jefferson. Later because of the promises in these letters and because of a recognition of the principle which had given rise to them, the Secretary of Foreign Affairs under the Constitution informed the Senate that in his opinion the faith of the nation was pledged to ratify the convention which ultimately had been concluded. And finally the Senate advised ratification in accordance with this opinion even though it was believed that the nation would be the loser by the treaty ratified.

[1] *Sen. Exec. Jour.*, I. 7–8.

[2] Moore, *International Law Digest*, V. 184–202, discusses thoroughly the principle involved, quoting Vattel and other older as well as modern American and European authorities, and the opinions of American statesmen on the subject. See also Foster, *The Practice of Diplomacy*, Ch. XIII.

Yet despite the scrupulous observance of the rule of international law in this instance, the later interpretation and application of the constitutional provision which divides the treaty-making power of the United States between the President and the Senate soon impelled the new state to demand exemption from the ancient principle. As long as the President negotiated treaties actually "by and with the advice and consent of the Senate" the United States possessed no better grounds than any other nation for declining to ratify, or for ratifying partially and conditionally, agreements signed by its plenipotentiaries. But when the sanction of the Senate was sought only after negotiation had been completed, it became necessary for this country to secure the right of rejection or amendment if the constitutional powers of the Senate were to amount to more than an empty form. There was, then, an intimate relation between the manner in which the Senate was to exercise its treaty-making powers and the position of the United States with reference to the principle of international law involved. The ratification of the French consular convention illustrates the position of the Senate at the outset.

CHAPTER II

DEVELOPMENT OF TREATY-MAKING POWER THROUGH ACTION ON TREATIES WITH INDIAN TRIBES, 1789–1795

DURING the early nineties the Senate played an active part in negotiations which were in progress between the United States and Great Britain, Algiers, and France. None of the resulting treaties came before it for final action, however, until 1795, while in the meantime the treaty-making power was being vigorously exercised in concluding agreements between the United States and various Indian tribes.[1]

TREATIES OF FORT HARMAR

The first of these agreements were the two treaties of Fort Harmar submitted to the Senate on May 25, 1789. The consideration of the problems which arose in connection with these treaties occupied the attention of the Senate at intervals throughout practically all of the first session of Congress, and in the end it withheld its advice and consent to the ratification of one of them. In the meantime, however,

[1] Butler, *The Treaty-Making Power of the United States*, II. 203, and Ch. XIV, *passim*, discusses treaties with Indian tribes; also Burr, *The Treaty-Making Power of the United States*, pp. 383–384, considers the constitutional and legal status of treaties with Indian tribes.

11

one question had been definitely decided — namely, that the advice and consent of the Senate should be given to the ratification of treaties with Indian tribes in the same form as to treaties with foreign nations. The circumstances in which this decision was reached reveal how both the President and the Senate were feeling their way carefully and thoughtfully in the determination of the technique of treaty-making.

The papers which General Knox, under whose superintendence the business had been transacted, laid before the Senate included his report to the President, explaining the circumstances under which the treaties had been negotiated and signed. In this report the Secretary suggested the necessity, on constitutional grounds, of an explanation of the reservation in the treaty with the Six Nations of six square miles around the Fort at Oswego, which reservation was within the territory of the State of New York. He concluded by observing, "That, if this explanation should be made, and the Senate of the United States should concur in their approbation of the said treaties, it might be proper that the same should be ratified and published, with a proclamation enjoining the observance thereof." Two documents accompanied the report, No. 1 being a representation to the old Congress against the treaties superseded, while No. 2 was a copy of the instructions under which the new treaties were negotiated.[1]

It was not until June 12 that the Senate found time to turn its attention to these treaties. On

[1] *Sen. Exec. Jour.*, I. 3–5.

that day they were considered and put in charge of a committee of three, Few, Read, and Henry.[1] Two months later the committee reported:[2]

That the Governor of the Western Territory, on the 9th day of January, 1789, at Fort Harmar, entered into two treaties, one with the sachems and warriors of the Six Nations, the Mohawks excepted, the other with the sachems and warriors of the Wyandot, Delaware, Ottawa, Chippewa, Pattawattima, and Sacs nations — that those treaties were made in pursuance of the powers and instructions heretofore given to the said Governor by the late Congress, and are a confirmation of the Treaties of Ft. Stanwix, in October, 1784, and of Ft. McIntosh, in January, 1785, and contain a more formal and regular conveyance to the United States of the Indian claims to the lands yielded to these States by the said treaties of 1784 and 1785.

Your Committee, therefore, submit the following resolution, viz:

That the treaties concluded at Ft. Harmar, on the 9th day of January, 1789 between Arthur St. Clair, Esq., Governor of the Western Territory, on the part of the United States, and the sachems and warriors of the Six Nations, (the Mohawks excepted,) . . . and the sachems and warriors of the Wyandot . . . and Sacs nations, be accepted; and that the President of the United States be advised to execute and enjoin an observance of the same.[3]

Seemingly the committee felt it to be a most important part of its duty to determine whether the treaties referred to it were in accord with the instructions under which they were negotiated, a feeling shared by most of the early committees on treaties. And it thought proper, also, to follow closely, in the form of the resolution, the lead given

[1] *Sen. Exec. Jour.*, I. 6.　　[2] *Ibid.*, p. 17.　　[3] *Ibid.*, p. 24.

in the last clause of General Knox's report to the
President.

After consideration this report was allowed to lie
over until September 8, when a resolution was
adopted advising the President "to execute and
enjoin an observance of" the treaty with the Wyandots and other tribes. No mention was made in
the resolution of the treaty with the Six Nations,
although it is recorded in the journal that both
were considered.[1] The reason for the failure of the
Senate to act on this treaty soon appeared.

An attested copy of the resolution adopted having
been laid before the President, the Senate soon received a further communication from him on the
subject, again delivered by General Knox, who
meanwhile had been appointed the first Secretary
of War under the new government.[2] In this message Washington expressed the opinion that treaties
with Indian tribes should be ratified under the
same procedure as was intended to be followed with
reference to foreign treaties, although it is clear that
he did not think that such ratification was required
by the Constitution. He put the matter squarely
up to the Senate, however, in these words: "It
strikes me that this point should be well considered
and settled, so that our national proceedings, in
this respect, may become uniform, and be directed
by fixed and stable principles." Following this
general statement is a paragraph which reveals how
in the original submission he had intentionally left
to the Senate a free field in suggesting the procedure
to be followed. Washington said:

[1] *Sen. Exec. Jour.*, I. 25.   [2] *Ibid.*, pp. 26, 27.

The treaties with certain Indian Nations, which were laid before you with my message of the 25th of May last, suggested two questions to my mind, viz: 1st, Whether those treaties were to be considered as perfected, and consequently as obligatory, without being ratified? If not, then 2dly, Whether both, or either, and which of them, ought to be ratified? On these questions I request your opinion and advice.[1]

The Senate committed this message to another committee of three members, Carroll, King, and Read.[2]

In its report, presented next day, this committee expressed the opinion that, in view of the fact that in the past Indian treaties had been considered as fully completed upon signature and without solemn ratification, the formal ratification of the treaty with the Wyandots and other Indian nations was not expedient or necessary; and accordingly that the resolution of the Senate of September 8 was all that was required in the case, since it authorized the President to "enjoin a due observance" of the treaty. The committee further reported that as to the treaty with the Six Nations, "from particular circumstances affecting the ceded lands, the Senate did not judge it expedient to pass any act concerning the same."[3]

This report, however, proved to be unacceptable to the majority of the Senate and in the end Washington's suggestion as to formal ratification was adopted. On the following Tuesday, September 22, a resolution was passed ratifying in form the treaty with the Wyandots et al.; but in the case of the treaty with the Six Nations the Senate declined to

[1] Sen. Exec. Jour., I. 27.   [2] Ibid.   [3] Ibid., pp. 27, 28.

accept any responsibility either of a positive or of a negative sort. As the journal puts it, "And it being suggested that the treaty concluded at Fort Harmar . . . may be construed to prejudice the claims of the States of Massachusetts and New York, and of the grantees under the said states respectively. *Ordered*, That the consideration thereof be postponed until next session of Senate." [1] The Senate evidently continued to deem it inexpedient to act in this delicate matter, for no record of any further consideration appears in the journals of the next or of subsequent sessions.

Thus by a process of give and take the Senate and the executive worked out the problems imposed by their joint functions. The direct and personal contact which still marked their relations in treaty-making is illustrated by the appearance before the Senate of General Knox as the head of the executive department concerned.

TREATY WITH THE CREEK INDIANS, 1789

Coincidently with the discussion over the ratification of the Fort Harmar treaties arose the question of the proper rôle of the Senate in the negotiation of such agreements and of foreign treaties. Very probably the early Senators examined the treaty clause itself to see what light it might throw upon this question. This clause appears in the Constitution as follows: "He [the President] shall have power, by and with the advice and consent of the Senate, to make treaties,

[1] *Ibid.*, p. 28.

provided two-thirds of the Senators present concur; and he shall nominate, and by and with the advice and consent of the Senate, shall appoint ambassadors," etc.

Senator Henry Cabot Lodge, in our own day, has quoted the provision in regard to nominations and appointments, in order to define more fully the preceding one relating to treaties.[1] And he points out that it is

well to note that the carefully phrased section gives the President absolute and unrestricted right to nominate, and the Senate can only advise and consent to the appointment of, a given person. All right to interfere in the remotest degree with the power of nomination and the consequent power of selection is wholly taken from the Senate. Very different is the wording of the treaty clause. There the words "by and with the advice and consent of" come in after the words "shall have power" and before the power referred to is defined. The "advice and consent of the Senate" are therefore coextensive with the "power" conferred on the President, which is "to make treaties," and apply to the entire process of treaty-making.

Senator Lodge concludes that except for their want of authority to send or to receive ambassadors or ministers and their consequent inability to initiate a negotiation the Senate, under the language of the Constitution and in the intent of the framers, stands on a perfect equality with the President in the making of treaties. That this was the opinion of the first executive and of the early Senates is clearly disclosed in their handling of Indian and

[1] Lodge, "The Treaty-Making Powers of the Senate," in *A Fighting Frigate and Other Essays and Addresses*, pp. 231–232.

foreign affairs, which also reveals the reasons why the Senate soon ceased to participate directly in treaty-making during the period of negotiation. It being then generally assumed, however, that the President would at times discuss personally with the Senate the subjects of nominations to office and of treaties, the question as to where and how, and incidentally whether, these consultations should take place soon came up for decision. To this end, early in August, 1789, Senators Izard, King, and Carroll were appointed as a committee, "to wait upon the President of the United States and confer with him on the mode of communication proper to be pursued between him and the Senate, in the formation of treaties, and making appointments to offices." [1]

Two days after their appointment, August 8, these gentlemen conferred with the President, and on the tenth they held a second meeting at which his sentiments were finally expressed.[2] Washington evidently felt that nominations should be made by written messages, but that personal conferences were preferable in forming treaties. In the memorandum of his sentiments as expressed at the conference of August 8 he is recorded as having taken the position that,

In all matters respecting *Treaties*, oral communications seem indispensably necessary; because in these a variety of matters are contained, all of which not only require consideration, but some of them may undergo much dis-

---

[1] *Sen. Exec. Jour.*, I. 12, 16.
[2] Washington to Madison, Aug. 9, 1789, Washington's *Writings* (Ford ed.), XI. 415; Notes on conferences, *Ibid.*, 417–419.

cussion; to do which by written communications would be tedious without being satisfactory.[1]

And at the second conference he is reported to have stated his opinion as to the proper relations between the President and the Senate in treaty matters in these words:

> The President has power, by and with the advice and consent of the Senate, to make treaties and to appoint officers.
>
> The Senate, when this power is exercised, is evidently a council only to the President, however its concurrence may be to his acts. . . . In the appointment to offices, the agency of the Senate is purely executive, and they may be summoned to the President. In treaties, the agency is perhaps as much of a legislative nature, and the business may possibly be referred to their deliberations in their legislative chamber. The occasion for this distinction will be lessened if not destroyed, when a chamber shall be appropriated for the joint business of the President and the Senate.[2]

With reference to the manner of consultation the President observed,

> In other cases, again, as in treaties of a complicated nature, it may happen, that he will send his propositions in writing, and consult the Senate in person after time shall have been allowed for consideration.

And finally, because any hard and fast rule of procedure would be very likely to prove unfortunate, he recommended that

> the Senate should accomodate their rules to the uncertainty of the particular mode and place, that may be

[1] Washington to Madison, Aug. 9, 1789, Washington's *Writings* (Ford ed.), XI. 415; Notes on conferences, *Ibid.*, 417–419.

[2] *Ibid.*

preferred, providing for the reception of either oral or written propositions, and for giving their consent and advice in either the *presence* or *absence* of the President, leaving him free to use the mode and place, that may be found most eligible and accordant with other business, which may be before him at the time.[1]

The views of the President evidently were concurred in by the committee, for its report, presented and adopted August 21, made provision for meetings of the Senate and the President under procedure acceptable to both of them, but left it to the President to decide in each particular case whether the business should be transacted orally or by written messages.[2]

The judgment of the President and of the Senate as to the desirability and practicability of personal conferences upon treaties was soon to be put to the test of practical application. The very day

[1] Washington to Madison, Aug. 9, 1789, Washington's *Writings* (Ford ed.), XI. 415; Notes on conferences, *Ibid.*, 417–419.

[2] This report was adopted in the following form: "*Resolved*, That when nominations shall be made in writing by the President of the United States to the Senate, a future day shall be assigned, unless the Senate unanimously direct otherwise, for taking them into consideration. That when the President of the United States shall meet the Senate in the Senate Chamber, the President of the Senate shall have a chair on the floor, be considered as the head of the Senate, and his chair shall be assigned to the President of the United States. That when the Senate shall be convened by the President of the United States to any other place, the President of the Senate and Senators shall attend at the place appointed. The Secretary of the Senate shall also attend to take the minutes of the Senate.

"That all questions shall be put by the President of the Senate, either in the presence or the absence of the President of the United States; and the Senators shall signify their assent or dissent by answering, viva voce, ay or no." *Sen. Exec. Jour.*, I. 19.

upon which the rule of procedure was adopted the Senate received the following communication from Washington, delivered by Tobias Lear, his private secretary:

Gentlemen of the Senate: The President of the United States will meet the Senate, in the Senate Chamber, at half past eleven o'clock, tomorrow, to advise with them on the terms of a treaty to be negotiated with the Southern Indians.[1]

The general problem which Washington sought to solve by a treaty already was well known to the Senate, and, indeed, to members of both houses, and to the country. Two weeks previously he had laid before the Senate the facts concerning the disputes between Georgia and other states and certain powerful tribes of Indians within the limits of the Union, and had pointed out the necessity for the interposition of the general government between the disputants. He had also suggested that if it should be the judgment of Congress that a treaty should be made with the Southern Indians, it might be expedient to institute a temporary commission of three persons, for that purpose, whose authority should expire with the occasion.[2] Congress had responded by providing for the expenses of the proposed negotiations,[3] and on August 21 the appointment of the three commissioners had been confirmed.[4]

---

[1] Richardson, *Compilation of the Messages and Papers of the Presidents*, I. 61. Phillips, *Georgia and States Rights*, Ch. II, discusses the negotiation, ratification and political aspects of this treaty.

[2] *Annals of Congress*, 1789–1791, I. 59–60.   [3] *Ibid.*, p. 65.

[4] *Sen. Exec. Jour.*, I. 19.

From the standpoint of this study the interest of the two conferences which followed between the President and his constitutional advisers does not lie in the measures which they agreed should be taken to solve the problem of the moment. In their effect upon the treaty-making powers of the Senate, the meetings are of importance because they were so uncomfortable to both parties that Washington never again personally consulted with the Senate about treaties, or, indeed, upon any other subject — an example which has been followed by every one of his successors.[1]

After explaining the points at issue between Georgia and North Carolina and the Indian tribes, and emphasizing the importance to those states and to the union of effecting a speedy settlement of the difficulty, the President asked the advice of the Senate upon the instructions to be given to the commissioners of the United States. This he did by submitting seven propositions prefaced by these words:

As it is necessary that certain principles should be fixed, previously to forming instructions for the Commissioners, the following questions, arising out of the foregoing communications, are stated by the President of the United States, and the advice of the Senate requested thereon.

Then followed the seven specific questions, covering the entire instructions to the commissioners and designed to secure the advice of the Senate upon what action should be taken by them in every alternative that might arise during the negotiation.

[1] The appearance of President Wilson before the Senate, July 10, 1919, was not for consultation.

The questions were taken up seriatim and discussed by the Senators, the President, and General Knox. Some of the propositions were assented to or dissented from as they had been presented, while others were modified. The proceeding took the greater part of two legislative days, but finally the "advice and consent" of the Senate had been given to a course of action intended to cover all possible contingencies.[1] The instructions later issued to the commissioners conform strictly to this advice.[2]

There is little in the pages of the *Senate Executive Journal* to indicate that this method of procedure was not satisfactory to all parties concerned. Fortunately, however, we are permitted a more intimate view of these conferences in the familiar diary of Senator Maclay,[3] a view which makes it seem very likely that Washington did say when he left the Senate chamber that he would " be damned " if he ever came there again.[4]

[1] *Sen. Exec. Jour.*, I. 20–24.

[2] *American State Papers, Indian Affairs*, I. 65–68.

[3] *Journal of William Maclay*, pp. 128–133.

[4] This story, which John Quincy Adams recounts in his diary, and which has often been repeated, is as follows:' "Mr. Crawford told twice over the story of President Washington's having at an early period of his administration gone to the Senate with a project of a treaty to be negotiated and been present at their deliberations upon it. They debated it and proposed alterations, so that when Washington left the Senate Chamber he said he would be damned if he ever went there again. And ever since that time treaties have been negotiated by the Executive *before* submitting them to the consideration of the Senate.

"The President said he had come into the Senate about eighteen months after the first organization of the present Government, and then heard that something like this had occurred.

" Crawford then repeated the story, varying the words, so as to

It is evident from Maclay's account that con-
straint and tension marked the conferences from
beginning to end. The entire proceeding must
have been felt to be unnatural, forced, and unsatisfactory. Maclay's own words graphically describe what occurred:

Senate met, and went on the Coasting bill. The
doorkeeper soon told us of the arrival of the President.
The President was introduced, and took our Vice-President's chair. He rose and told us bluntly that he had
called on us for our advice and consent to some propositions respecting the treaty to be held with the Southern
Indians. Said he had brought General Knox with him,
who was well acquainted with the business. He then
turned to General Knox, who was seated on the left of
the chair. General Knox handed him a paper, which he
handed to the President of the Senate, who was seated on
a chair on the floor to his right. Our Vice-President
hurried over the paper. Carriages were driving past,
and such a noise, I could tell it was something about
"Indians," but was not master of one sentence of it.
Signs were made to the doorkeeper to shut down the
sashes. Seven heads, as we have since learned, were
stated at the end of the paper which the Senate were to
give their advice and consent to. They were so framed
that it could not be done by aye or no.
The President told us that a paper from an agent of
the Cherokees was given to him just as he was coming to
the Hall. He motioned to General Knox for it, and
handed it to the President of the Senate. It was read.
It complained hard of the unjust treatment of the people

say that Washington swore he would never go to the Senate again."
Memoirs of John Quincy Adams, VI. 427.
It is evident that the story had been told to Crawford by President Monroe. This was not the last treaty that was submitted
to the Senate before negotiation, although it is the only occasion
on which such submission was made orally by the President.

of North Carolina, etc., their violation of treaties, etc. Our Vice-President now read off the first article, to which our advice and consent were requested. It referred back principally to some statements in the body of the writing which had been read.

Mr. Morris rose. Said the noise of carriages had been so great that he really could not say that he had heard the body of the paper which had been read, and prayed that it might be read again. It was so [read]. It was no sooner read than our Vice-President immediately read the first head over again, and put the question: Do you advise and consent, etc.? There was a dead pause. Mr. Morris whispered to me, "We will see who will venture to break silence first." Our Vice-President was proceeding, "As many as —"

I rose reluctantly, indeed, and, from the length of the pause, the hint given by Mr. Morris, and the proceeding of our Vice-President, it appeared to me that if I did not no other one would, and we should have these advices and consents ravished, in a degree, from us.

Maclay then called for the reading of the treaties and the other documents referred to in the message of the President. Whether or not he saw only what he expected, we have no means of knowing. But he records that he then "cast an eye at the President of the United States. I saw he wore an aspect of stern displeasure." Other senators participated in the discussion and called for the reading of particular papers. As our diarist laconically puts it, "The business labored with the Senate." The first two articles were postponed and a long discussion over the merits of the third article followed, in which Ellsworth, Lee, and Izard discoursed learnedly until Morris "at last informed the disputants that they were debating a subject that was actually postponed." This statement gave rise to a parlimentary wrangle which ended in repassing the motion to postpone.

At this point Morris, following a whispered suggestion from his colleague, rose and moved that all the papers be committed. More debate then followed, in which Butler made his pertinent and oft-quoted statement that the Senate was acting as a council, and that no council ever committed anything. Maclay himself concluded the debate by what must have been a stilted and pedantic dissertation upon the advantages of doing business by committees. This apparently brought Washington to his feet in exasperation, for Maclay states:

As I sat down, the President of the United States started up in a violent fret. "*This defeats every purpose of my coming here,*" were the first words he said. He then went on that he had brought his Secretary of War with him to give every necessary information; that the Secretary knew all about the business, and yet he was delayed and could not go on with the matter. He cooled, however, by degrees.

The entry in the diary continues to describe the whole of the two conferences. But this is enough, perhaps, to explain why Washington changed his mind about the desirability of oral communications where treaties were concerned. As the Senate increased in size the inherent difficulties of personal consultation became greater, and for this and other reasons it is not surprising that none of his successors has ever repeated an experiment which Washington found to be so unpleasant.

In its inception, then, the Creek treaty (1) indicates that the President considered it at least desirable to secure in advance the detailed and specific advice of the Senate as to the instructions under which treaties were to be negotiated; (2) it shows that he believed personal consultation to be the most advantageous method of taking this advice; and (3) it demonstrates that such procedure was found to be unsatisfactory both to the President and to the Senate.

But even after having consulted the Senate upon the instructions to be given to the commissioners, Washington did not take the whole negotiation into his own hands and ignore the Senate until the completed treaty was laid before it. Some four months later, January 11, 1790, he communicated to the Senate the instructions which he had given to the commissioners and their report upon the negotiation, in which the Creeks had refused to conclude a treaty.[1]

In the following summer representatives of the Creek Nation came to New York for further negotiation, and in August Washington informed the Senate that the "adjustment of the terms of the treaty is far advanced."[2] He also submitted a

---

[1] *American State Papers, Indian Affairs,* I. 59. The entry in the journal of the Senate is, "*Ordered,* That the communication from the President of the United States be deferred for consideration." *Sen. Exec. Jour.,* I. 36.

Maclay, however, records that "a considerable part of the day" was spent in reading the proceedings of the commissioners. *Journal of William Maclay,* pp. 174–5. The papers submitted cover twenty pages in the folio volume — some 48,000 words.

[2] *Sen. Exec. Jour.,* I. 55–56.

proposed secret article to be added to the treaty
for the purpose of transferring the trade of the
Indians from English and Spanish to American
control. After consideration it was,

Resolved, That the Senate do advise and consent to
the execution of the secret article referred to in the message, and that the blank in said article be filed in with
the words, "the President of the United States." [1]

On August 6 the Senate was informed that the
negotiation had reached the point where the business might be conducted and concluded in form.
General Knox was nominated to conclude the treaty
and the nomination was at once confirmed. On
the following day the signed treaty was transmitted
with a message explaining its salient features and
offering to have communicated to the Senate such
papers, documents, and information concerning it as
might be required.[2]

By taking their advice on the instructions to the
commissioners, by informing them of the progress
of the negotiation, and by securing their formal
advice and consent to the secret article, the President would seem to have made the agreement with
the Creeks as much the Senate's treaty as his own.
Neither party, however, seems to have assumed that
the advice and consent which the Senate had given
to the negotiation of the treaty in accordance with
certain definite propositions constituted the whole
of the senatorial assent contemplated by the Constitution. Article XIV of the treaty specifically provides that, "This treaty shall take effect and be

---

[1] *Sen. Exec. Jour.*, I. 56.   [2] *Ibid.*, pp. 57–58.

obligatory on the contracting parties, as soon as the same shall have been ratified by the President of the United States, with the advice and consent of the Senate of the United States." [1]

The message of the President and the treaty were read in the Senate on the Saturday upon which they were received and it was then ordered that they lie for consideration. Upon taking the matter up the following Monday, a motion, supported by those who opposed the treaty, to refer it to a select committee failed by an eight to ten yea and nay vote. [2]

It was then proposed:

That, on the final question, when the advice and consent of the Senate is requested, any member shall have a right to enter his protest or dissent on the journal, with reasons in support of such dissent; provided the same be offered within two days after the determination on such final question.

This motion failed, fifteen to four. [3]

Three days later the treaty was again taken up and by a yea and nay vote of fifteen to four the advice and consent of the Senate given in the following form:

"Resolved, (two thirds of the Senators present concurring therein,) That the Senate do consent to the aforesaid treaty, and do advise the President of the United States to ratify the same." [4]

[1] Indian Affairs, Laws and Treaties, II. 22, Sen. Doc., vol. 35, no. 452, ser. no. 4254, 57th Cong., 1st Sess.

[2] Sen. Exec. Jour., I. 59.   [3] Ibid.

[4] Sen. Exec. Jour., I. 61, 62. It seems to have been merely a coincidence that the motion to allow members to enter upon the journal their protests or dissents from the action of the Senate in

TREATY WITH THE CHEROKEE INDIANS

On the day before the final action of the Senate on the Creek agreement a message was transmitted to them by Washington asking their advice and consent to the principal terms of a proposed treaty to settle somewhat similar difficulties which had arisen between Georgia and the Cherokees. The United States was involved in the matter as a result of its treaty of November, 1785, with this tribe of Indians. The President recited that by this agreement, known as the Treaty of Hopewell, the Cherokees had placed themselves under the protection of the United States, that a boundary had been assigned to them, and that the whites on the frontier had openly violated this boundary by settling on the Cherokee lands, and had ignored the proclamation of the Congress of 1788 ordering them out. In view of the facts Washington felt it to be his duty either to enforce the old treaty or to negotiate a new one. He therefore stated the following questions and requested the advice of the Senate thereon:

1st. Is it the judgment of the Senate that overtures shall be made to the Cherokees to arrange a new boundary so as to embrace the settlements made by the white people since the treaty of Hopewell, in November, 1785?

giving its advice and consent failed by the same vote by which the treaty itself passed. Butler of South Carolina and Gunn of Georgia voted for the first proposition, and against the resolution of advice and consent. But Gunn's colleague Few, who also opposed the ratification of the treaty, voted nay on the motion to allow dissenting opinions to be recorded in the journal. Both Izard of North Carolina and Lee of Virginia, who supported the latter proposition, voted in favor of the ratification of the treaty.

2d. If so, shall compensation, to the amount of —— dollars annually, or of —— dollars in gross, be made to the Cherokees for the land they shall relinquish, holding the occupiers of the land accountable to the United States for its value?

3d. Shall the United States stipulate solemnly to guarantee the new boundary which may be arranged? [1]

Two differences are to be noticed between these questions and those put to the Senate in the case of the Creek treaty. The latter were propounded by Washington in person; the former were presented in writing by the President's secretary and nothing was said about either Washington or General Knox attending or furnishing any information other than that contained in the message itself. Also, the questions are of a more general nature, and do not attempt to cover the various alternatives which might be expected to arise in the negotiation. Further, the questions were answered in a different manner, the Senate discussing the whole matter at will and then summing up its conclusions in two brief resolutions. In replying to the first of the three questions, the Senate left it to the President either to cause the treaty of Hopewell to be carried into execution or to enter into arrangements with the Cherokees for a further cession of territory. The alternative of an annual payment was recommended, the amount being limited to $1000, and the condition was laid down that the occupiers of the land should be confirmed in possession only by a compliance with such terms as Congress might afterwards prescribe. And, finally, it was

[1] *Sen. Exec. Jour.*, I. 61.

Resolved, In case a new, or other boundary than that
stipulated by the treaty of Hopewell, shall be concluded
with the Cherokee Indians, that the Senate do advise
and consent solemnly to guarantee the same.[1]

This last resolution was of a type adopted several
times by the Senate during the early administrations.
Later Senates did not bind themselves thus in advance, and would have deemed such a promise incompatible with their right to withhold their assent
from any provision of a treaty submitted to them.
What would have been the position of the Senate
had the President concluded a treaty with the
Cherokees creating a boundary that threatened to
bring Georgia into serious conflict with the federal
government? How far would it have held itself
to be bound by this resolution, — particularly if
the balance of power had passed from one party to
the other in the interim? These questions did not
then arise, but it is inevitable that sooner or later
some such situation would have been created had
this practice become established. The resolution,
however, is but another expression of the general
principle which governed in the ratification of the
French consular convention, namely, that a nation
is bound to accept treaties signed by its plenipotentiaries, provided the latter have followed their
instructions. It will be perceived that at this time
both the Senate and the President were acting in
accordance with the first of the two alternatives
suggested in that connection — that is, under the
theory that the Senate should participate in deciding
what instructions should be given to the negotiator,

[1] *Sen. Exec. Jour.*, I. 61.

and then be bound to the same extent as was the President to ratify the resulting treaty.

The treaty which was concluded with the Cherokees in accordance with the advice given by the Senate on August 11, 1790, was submitted to the Senate more than a year later, two days after the meeting of the first session of the second Congress. With it were transmitted the papers which related to the negotiations, amounting in all to some 7000 words.[1] The message, treaty, and papers were read and ordered to lie for consideration,[2] and a week later were referred to a committee composed of Hawkins, Cabot, and Sherman.[3] This committee reported, in part, as follows:

That they have examined the said treaty, and find it strictly conformable to the instructions given by the President of the United States.

That these instructions were founded on the advice and consent of the Senate, of the 11th of August, 1790.

That the stipulations in the 14th article are similar to those gratuitously promised to the Creeks; and although they form an excess to the sum limited in the resolution aforesaid, yet from the beneficial effects likely to be produced thereby, cannot be objectionable.

The committee briefly described the new boundary and expressed the opinion that the treaty should be ratified, whereupon the Senate agreed to the report and formally gave its consent to the treaty and advised its ratification by the President.[4]

Thus in the treaty with the Cherokees as in that

---

[1] *Sen. Exec. Jour.*, I. 85; *Am. State Papers, Indian Affairs*, I. 123–129.

[2] *Sen. Exec. Jour.*, I. 85.   [3] *Ibid.*, pp. 85, 88.

[4] *Ibid.* pp. 88, 89.

with the Creeks the Senate was asked in advance to give its advice as to the terms to be proposed by the commissioners of the United States. The principal difference in the procedure was that in the earlier case this advice was given during a personal consultation between the President and the Senate, while the details of the later negotiation were settled by messages between the two. The procedure of the Senate subsequently to the signature of the treaty was much the same in each case, except that the Cherokee agreement was referred to a committee, while no such reference was made when the question of the ratification of the Creek treaty was being considered.

It should be observed that in this, as in other cases, the report of the committee emphasized the general conformity of the treaty with the advice and consent of the Senate given prior to the negotiation, and that evidently it was considered that such conformity laid upon the Senate an obligation to assent to ratification. The single stipulation not conforming with this prior consent was noted by the committee but was declared to be unobjectionable.

OTHER TREATIES WITH INDIAN TRIBES

In 1794 the Senate for the first time exercised its prerogative of refusing to consent to the ratification of a treaty negotiated by the executive. In 1793 General Putnam had concluded a treaty of peace and friendship with the Wabash and Illinois Indians, acting under instructions about which the Senate never had been consulted. The result of his negotiations was submitted to the Senate February 13, 1793, with a message in which the President adopted a course which frequently was followed in later years — that is, he himself suggested the ratification of the treaty with an amendment. In making this suggestion he said:

After the Senate shall have considered this treaty, I request that they would give me their advice whether the same shall be ratified and confirmed; and, if to be ratified and confirmed, whether it would not be proper, in order to prevent any misconception hereafter of the fourth article, to guard, in the ratification, the exclusive pre-emption of the United States to the land of the said Indians.[1]

In this instance, however, the presidential suggestion did not meet with favor in the Senate. After that body had considered the treaty upon three separate occasions, the whole matter was referred to a committee of which Burr was chairman.[2] The report of this committee, which was adopted, recommended that further consideration of the treaty be postponed until the next session of Congress, and that in the meantime the President be requested to cause an explanatory article to be negotiated with the Indians, reserving the preëmptive

---

[1] The fourth article of this treaty was as follows: "The United States solemnly guaranty to the Wabash, and the Illinois nations, or tribes of Indians, all the lands to which they have just claim; and no part shall ever be taken from them, but by a fair purchase, and to their satisfaction. That the lands originally belonged to the Indians; it is theirs and theirs only. That they have a right to sell, and a right to refuse to sell. And that the United States will protect them in their said just rights." *Am. State Papers, Indian Relations*, I. 338.

[2] *Sen. Exec. Jour.*, I. 128.

rights in the Indian lands to the United States, as he had suggested in his message.[1]

Before this could be done, however, most of the chiefs who had signed the treaty had died of small-pox, and early in the next session the President reported that while his instructions to other commissioners had been modified to protect the rights in question in the future, nothing could be effected towards modifying this particular treaty.[2] This brought the treaty and Washington's original suggestion once more before the Senate. Upon the failure of an attempt again to postpone action until the next session, with a renewal of the suggestion that the President cause an explanation to the fourth article to be negotiated, the friends of the treaty sought to secure ratification with a proviso such as that originally proposed by Washington. They failed in this, however, and the matter finally was concluded by the rejection by a vote of twenty-one to four of a simple resolution of advice and consent to ratification.[3] It is evident from the votes that a large minority of the Senate was ready to give the President another opportunity to modify the treaty and perhaps to accept it with the suggested proviso. But only four of this minority, Cabot, Ellsworth, Foster, and Strong, voted for the resolution to accept the treaty as it stood.[4] Thus the Senate for the first time declined to give its advice and consent to the ratification of a treaty negotiated under the direction of the President.

[1] *Sen. Exec. Jour.*, I. 134–135.
[2] *Ibid.*, p. 145; *Am. State Papers, Indian Affairs*, I. 470.
[3] *Ibid.*, pp. 145–6.　　　　　　　[4] *Ibid.*

The rejection is especially notable because the treaty from which assent was withheld was one of the first to be negotiated by the executive independently of the Senate. On this account the position of the Senate with reference to ratification was likewise one of independence — an independence which was manifested first in the refusal to accede to the presidential suggestion that a conditional ratification be resorted to, and second in the rejection of the treaty when the suggested negotiation had failed to remove or alter the provision to which exception had been taken.

Procedure upon all but one of the remaining Indian treaties considered by the Senate during Washington's administrations may be disposed of in comparatively few words.[1] Four of these were signed by executive agents without any consultation with the Senate either before or during negotiation. In no case did the latter body take exception to being thus ignored, the ratification of each of the treaties being consented to with little opposition. Light is thrown upon the position taken by Washington on this point by certain facts in connection with the Treaty of Greenville with the Indians northwest of the Ohio. On February

---

[1] The following additional treaties were before the Senate during Washington's administration: Six Nations, 1794 — *Sen. Exec. Jour.*, I. 168–170; Oneidas and Others, 1794 — *Ibid.*; Indians Northwest of the Ohio (Greenville), 1795 — *Ibid.*, pp. 193 -197; Seven Nations of Canada, 1797 — *Ibid.*, pp. 219–220; Additional Article, Cherokee Nation (1791), 1792 — *Ibid.*, pp. 98–99; Additional Article, Cherokee Nation (Holston Treaty), 1794 — *Ibid.*, pp. 168–170; Additional Article, Five Nations, 1792 — *Ibid.*, p. 116.

The treaty with the Creek Nation, 1796, is discussed on pp. 95–107 below.

25, 1793, the three heads of departments and the Attorney General were asked four questions as to the kind of treaty that should be sought, and as to the powers in the matter possessed respectively by the executive alone and by the executive and the Senate. In response to the fourth question, whether the Senate should previously be consulted upon the extent of the relinquishments of land which should be made to the Indians in order to secure peace, the cabinet expressed the unanimous opinion that it would be better not to consult them previously. The following paragraph from a memorandum made by Jefferson the day after the conference explains why the cabinet gave this advice: "Fourth question. We all thought if the Senate should be consulted, and consequently apprised of our line, it would become known to Hammond,[1] and we would lose all chance of saving anything more than our ultimatum." This advice was followed and the first official intimation given to the Senate of the instructions under which the resulting treaty was negotiated was received when the completed agreement was laid before them.

It is only necessary to compare the procedure in this case with that upon two earlier Indian treaties to appreciate the extent to which the practical forces of politics were changing the manner in which the President and the Senate exercised their function of treaty-making. Before approaching the Creeks in 1789 Washington personally appeared before the Senate, and after prolonged consultation received in advance their advice and consent in detail to

[1] George Hammond, British minister to the United States.

instructions which embodied every provision of the proposed treaty. A year later, as the Senate was about to consent to the ratification of the Creek treaty, he laid before them for their formal sanction, this time by written message, the general propositions upon which he desired to base an agreement with the Cherokees. And finally, in 1793, when it became necessary to settle the problems arising out of Indian and British relations in the northwest, he decided from motives of expediency not to consult the Senate in any way until after the proposed treaty had been signed.

In addition to the new treaties with Indian tribes which were made during Washington's administration, it was found advisable in 1792 to provide for increasing the annuities paid to the Five Nations, under the Treaty of 1789,[1] and to the Cherokees, under the treaty of 1791,[2] from $1000 to $1500. In each case the President explained to the Senate the reasons for granting the increase and asked and received its advice as to the negotiation of the additional article providing for it, after which the articles were signed and proclaimed without any further question.

[1] *Sen. Exec. Jour.*, I. 116.   [2] *Ibid.*, pp. 98–99.

CHAPTER III

THE TREATIES WITH ALGIERS AND SPAIN, 1790–1796

DURING Washington's administrations the Senate was called upon to participate in making the Jay treaty, the treaty of peace and amity with the Dey of Algiers, concluded in September, 1795, and the Spanish treaty signed a month later. In each case it played an important part not only in the ratification of the treaty, but also during its negotiation. And as these three treaties were the result of much of the diplomacy of the first eight years of our national existence, it follows that the Senate exercised a constant influence over our foreign relations during this period. Although these negotiations will be taken up separately, it should be borne in mind that they were being carried on simultaneously.[1]

THE TREATY WITH ALGIERS, 1795

In his second annual address, delivered December 8, 1790, Washington briefly directed the attention of

[1] The relations with England leading up to the Jay Treaty were first considered in the Senate February 9, 1790; the treaty was submitted to the Senate for its advice and consent June 8, 1795, which advice and consent were given, conditionally, June 24, 1795; for the treaty with Algiers the dates were December 30, 1790, February 15, 1796, March 2, 1796; for the Spanish treaty, January 11, 1792, February 26, 1796, March 3, 1796.

Congress to the distressed condition of American trade in the Mediterranean and recommended deliberations which might lead to its relief and protection.[1] A committee consisting of Langdon, Morris, King, Strong, and Ellsworth was appointed to consider the matter, and to it also was referred a message from Washington to Congress dated December 30, 1790, submitting a report from the Secretary of State setting forth the facts concerning the capture of twenty-one American seamen by the Algerines in 1785 and outlining the efforts since made by the government to ransom them at a reasonable price.[2] On December 30, also, another report of the Secretary of State on commerce in the Mediterranean was submitted to the House of Representatives and four days later was laid before the Senate. After thoroughly analyzing the situation Jefferson concluded that "Upon the whole, it rests with Congress to decide between war, tribute, and ransom, as the means of establishing our Mediterranean commerce."[3] In the same document Congress was informed that the death of the late Emperor of Morocco had made it necessary to obtain immediate recognition by his successor of the liberal treaty of 1787 with that power, a treaty necessary to our Atlantic as well as to our Mediterranean trade.[4] It will be seen, therefore, that the question of our Mediterranean commerce in-

---

[1] Richardson, *A Compilation of the Messages and Papers of the Presidents, 1789–1897*, I. 83. Cited below as Richardson, *Messages*.

[2] *American State Papers, Foreign Relations*, I. 100–104; *Annals of Congress, 1789–1791*, II. 1735, 1740–1741.

[3] *Am. State Papers, For. Rels.*, I. 105.   [4] *Ibid.*

volved three points: first, the ransoming or rescuing of the twenty-one seamen held captive by the Algerines; second, by force or by tribute securing our ships from further molestation; third, securing recognition by the new Emperor of Morocco of our treaty with that nation. The solution of this problem, or of any part of it, required the expenditure of money; and circumstances were such that if negotiations for a treaty with Algiers were resorted to the executive must be able to go to the Dey with cash in hand. Consequently both the executive and the Senate soon had to decide what would be the relations in this matter between themselves, respectively, and the House of Representatives, whose assent would be required for any appropriation.

Langdon's committee reported on January 6, 1791,[1] that the trade of the United States in the Mediterranean could be protected only by a naval force, and that it would be proper to resort to such force as soon as the state of the public finances would permit.[2] When, three weeks later, the Secretary of State transmitted another statement regarding the Algerine prisoners, this was referred to the same committee, whose report of the sixth was recommitted.[3] On February 1, this time in executive session, Langdon's committee was again heard from, now on the subject of the American captives and the Moroccan treaty. It reported a resolution:

---

[1] See page 41 above.

[2] *Annals of Congress*, 1789–1791, II. 1744; *Am. State Papers, For. Rels.*, I. 108.

[3] *Ibid.* p. 1749; *Am. State Papers, For. Rels.*, I. 116–120.

That the Senate advise and consent that the President of the United States take such measures as he may think necessary for the redemption of the citizens of the United States now in captivity at Algiers, provided the expense should not exceed forty thousand dollars; and also that measures be taken to confirm that treaty now existing between the United States and the Emperor of Morocco, provided that no greater sum than twenty thousand dollars be expended in that business.

With the exception of the proviso limiting the expense in the Moroccan business to $20,000 this resolution was adopted. At the same time another report of the committee, identical with that of January 6, was again recommitted.[1]

The resolution of advice was referred by the President to his Secretary of State, and by February 22 Jefferson had prepared a reply which was signed by Washington and submitted on that date.[2] The Senate was informed that the President would proceed to ransom the Algerine captives, and to secure recognition of the treaty with Morocco as soon as the necessary money had been appropriated by the legislature.[3] The matter was again referred to Langdon's committee, and on March 3 the Senate adopted the resolution which he reported to it, as follows:

Whereas, since the resolution of the Senate advising the President of the United States to take measures for the ransom of American captives at Algiers, large appropria-

---

[1] *Sen. Exec. Jour.*, I. 72–73. For the conclusion of the Morocco business, see pp. 52–53 below.

[2] *Writings of Thomas Jefferson*, IX. 331, 343–5; Jefferson to Madison, April 19, 1796 and enclosure.

[3] *Sen. Exec. Jour.*, I. 75.

tions of money have been made for the protection of the Western frontiers:

Resolved, That the Senate do advise and consent that the President of the United States suspend any operations under the said resolutions, for the ransom of said captives, until the situation of the treasury shall more clearly authorize the appropriation of money for that purpose.[1]

As this resolution was passed on the last day of the second session, it meant that the matter was to be held over until the next Congress.

Probably the Senate withdrew the "advice" which it had given a month previously not so much because the "situation of the treasury" had changed, as because Washington had intimated that he would not undertake the negotiations until the money required had been appropriated by Congress. The Senate was unwilling to ask the House of Representatives for an advance appropriation, and at the same time was not quite ready to advise the President to proceed without one.

Early in the first session of the second Congress the fate of the Algerine captives was again brought before the Senate by a petition of one of their number who had been privately ransomed. It was now ordered that all communications on the subject be referred to a committee to be composed of Butler, Langdon, Morris, King, and Strong, with instructions to report thereon.[2] On December 6 this committee recommended[3] that it be, "Resolved by the Senate of the United States, in their capacity as

---

[1] *Sen. Exec. Jour.,* I. 78.
[2] *Annals of Congress,* 1791–1793, I. 26.
[3] *Sen. Exec. Jour.,* I. 91.

Council of Advice," that if the President should secure a treaty with Algiers, Tunis, and Tripoli at an expense not exceeding $100,000 per year, and should ransom the Algerine captives at an expense of not more than $40,000 the Senate would advise and consent to the same and would also approve the expenditure of $5000 in the negotiation. It was recommended, further, that if no such treaty should be secured $2400 should be distributed annually among the families of the captives.[1]

This report was not accepted by the Senate but was made the basis of debate on the general question upon six different occasions during the following three months.[2] Early in March, 1791, it "was

---

[1] This report was as follows: "*Resolved by the Senate of the United States, in their capacity as Council of Advice*, That if the President of the United States shall enter into any treaty convention for the purpose of establishing and preserving a peace with the Regency of Algiers and with Tunis and Tripoli, at an expense not exceeding one hundred thousand dollars annually, for such term of years [as] shall be stipulated, and for the purpose of ransoming the citizens of the United States in captivity with the Algerines, 'at an expense not exceeding forty thousand dollars for the said ransom,' the Senate will advise and consent to the same, and ratify and approve any measures which the President of the United States shall take for accomplishing these measures to an amount not exceeding five thousand dollars, although such measures should prove unsuccessful.

"*Resolved*, That if a convention or treaty for the establishment of peace cannot be made with the Regency of Algiers the sum of two thousand four hundred dollars annually shall be distributed among the said captives or their families, as they may prefer, and in such proportion as the President of the United States shall order and direct during their captivity." *Compilation of Reports of the Committee on Foreign Relations, United States Senate, 1789–1901,* VIII. 6. Cited below as, *Compilation of Reports, Sen. Com. For. Rels.*

[2] *Sen. Exec. Jour.*, I. 91–100.

agreed to commit the report for the purpose of conferring with the President of the United States, on the subject matter thereof, to Mr. King, Mr. Morris, and Mr. Izard." [1] In Jefferson's notes on the conferences of this committee with Washington is to be found the real explanation of the failure of the Senate to act. "The President," he recorded,

had wished to redeem our captives at Algiers, and to make peace with them on paying an annual tribute. The Senate were willing to approve this, but unwilling to have the lower House applied to previously to furnish the money; they wished the President to take the money from the treasury, or open a loan for it. They thought that to consult the Representatives on one occasion, would give them a handle always to claim it, and would let them into a participation of the power of making treaties, which the Constitution had given exclusively to the President and the Senate. They said, too, that if the particular sum was voted by the Representatives, it would not be a secret.

Concerning Washington's position, Jefferson continued,

The President had no confidence in the Secrecy of the Senate, and did not choose to take money from the Treasury or to borrow. But he agreed he would enter into provisional treaties with the Algerines not to be binding on us until ratified here. [2]

[1] *Sen. Exec. Jour.*, p. 106.

[2] *The Writings of Thomas Jefferson* (Definitive edition), I. 294, 295, 305–309. "In this very case Mr. Izard made the communication to him, sitting next to him at table, on the one hand, while a lady (Mrs. McLane) was on his other hand, and the French minister next to her; and as Mr. Izard got on with his communication, his voice kept rising, and his stutter bolting the words out loudly at intervals, so that the minister might hear if he would. He said he had a great mind at one time to have got up, in order to put a stop to Mr. Izard."

Jefferson himself was opposed to "hazarding this transaction without the sanction of both Houses." "I had observed," he wrote,

that wherever the agency of either, or both Houses would be requisite subsequent to a treaty, to carry it into effect, it would be prudent to consult them previously if the occasion admitted. That thus it was, we were in the habit of consulting the Senate previously, when the occasion permitted because their subsequent ratification would be necessary. That there was the same reason for consulting the lower House previously, where they were to be called on afterwards, and especially in the case of money, as they held the purse strings, and would be jealous of them. However, he desired me to strike out the intimation that the seal would not be put till both Houses should have voted the money.[1]

No official record of the report of the committee of three has been preserved.[2] But whatever they may have recommended to the Senate, the outcome was that the appropriation which Washington desired was made by Congress before he proceeded

[1] *The Writings of Thomas Jefferson.* I. 294, 295, 305–309.

[2] A number of years later Jefferson found among his press copies the following, in his own handwriting: "The committee to report, that the President does not think that circumstances will justify, in the present instance, his entering into *absolute* engagements for the ransom of our captives in Algiers, nor calling for money from the Treasury, nor raising it by loan, without previous authority from *both branches* of the Legislature. April 9, 1792." In sending this paper to Madison in 1796 Jefferson stated that to the best of his recollection this was a minute that he had given privately to a member of the committee as expressing the substance of what had passed with the President, and that it probably had been used by the committee in its report to the Senate. However that may be, it is evident that the President adhered to his decision that the treaty should not be made until both houses should have voted the money. *The Writings of Thomas Jefferson*, IX. 331, 343–345.

with the negotiations. From the beginning the House had been kept informed of the status of our affairs in the Mediterranean as, indeed, it was throughout the entire negotiation of the treaty. As a result of this policy the representatives undoubtedly were fully conversant with the needs of the situation. In procuring the appropriation Washington, or Jefferson, must have acted through informal conferences with individual members; probably it is on this account that it now seems to be impossible to ascertain the manner in which they secured the passage of the bill.[1]

The House voted to make the appropriation, however, on the last day of the session, and the measure was at once presented to the Senate. Here the bill was read twice and referred to Morris, Cabot, and Ellsworth, who at the same time were asked to consider and report upon a message from the President on the Algerine matter. In this message Washington inquired if the Senate would approve a treaty providing for the ransom of the

[1] Tracing the matter as it appears in the Annals of Congress it is to be observed that on April 18 a petition was presented by two men ransomed from the Algerines by private means asking to be reimbursed for the amount of their ransom and their expenses from Algiers to the United States, and also that measures be taken to secure the ransom of the remaining prisoners. *Annals of Congress*, 1791–1793, p. 559.

The committee to which this petition was referred reported April 26, and their report was referred to "the Committee of the Whole House on the bill making certain appropriations therein mentioned." *Ibid.*, p. 580.

On May 7 this bill was considered in the Committee of the Whole, and ordered to be engrossed and read a third time on the morrow and on the eighth the first business recorded in the Annals is its passage. *Ibid.*, p. 600.

Algerine captives at a cost not to exceed $40,000, or if there was any greater or lesser sum which they would fix as the limit beyond which they would not approve the ransom. The same question was asked with reference to a treaty of peace at the cost of $25,000 down and a like sum to be paid annually during the continuance of the treaty. By adopting the resolution reported by the committee, the Senate promised to approve a treaty of peace providing for the payment of $25,000 upon signature and for an annual gift of $40,000 thereafter. The President was also informed that "in case such a treaty be concluded," the Senate would approve another agreement providing for the ransom of the captives at a cost not to exceed $25,000.[1]

At the same time the committee reported the House appropriation bill with an amendment, which was adopted by the Senate and agreed to by the House, the bill thus passing both chambers on the last day of the session. Section three of the act made the appropriation desired by the President by enacting

that a sum of fifty thousand dollars . . . be appropriated to defray any expense which may be incurred in relation to the intercourse between the United States and foreign nations, . . . to be applied under the direction of the President of the United States who, if necessary, is authorized to borrow, on the credit of the United States, the said sum of fifty thousand dollars; an account of the expenditure whereof as soon as may be, shall be laid before Congress.[2]

[1] *Sen. Exec. Jour.*, I. 122–123.
[2] *Statutes at Large of the United States of America*, I. 284–285 (Acts of 2d Cong., 1st Sess., Chap. XLI, Sec. 3).

The Senate thus had agreed to approve a treaty or treaties which called for a preliminary payment of $50,000, the exact amount appropriated at the same time to provide for intercourse between the United States and foreign nations. Evidently Morris, Cabot, and Ellsworth had proposed the Senate amendment to the House bill in order to make the appropriation coincide in amount with the sum fixed by the Senate as the limit for the preliminary payment. That the money was for this purpose cannot be doubted, for Jefferson in a subsequent report to Congress stated:

In order to enable the President to effect the objects of this (Senate) resolution, the Legislature, by their act of May 8th, 1792, c. 41, Sec. 3, appropriated a sum of fifty thousand dollars to defray any expense which might be incurred in relation to the intercourse between the United States and foreign nations.[1]

It is evident that in this transaction the Senate failed to maintain the position it had assumed. The point at issue was this: Has the President, upon the advice of the Senate, constitutional authority to draw money from the treasury or to borrow it on the credit of the United States in order to make the first payment on a treaty which he negotiates with the advice and consent of the Senate? And if so, is it the constitutional duty of Congress subsequently to appropriate the money so spent? The Senate answered both questions in the affirmative. The President and his Secretary of State seem not to have expressed any categorical opinion upon the abstract question; but

[1] *Am. State Papers, For. Rels.*, I. 290.

they declined to negotiate the treaty until the appropriation had been made. How far their position was based upon a consideration of the constitutional powers of the President, and to what degree the question of expediency determined their action we have no means of knowing. The course followed is characteristic of Washington's far-seeing caution in constitutional interpretation and in politics. Incidently, it left the principle at issue for the decision of the future.

The incident is an interesting revelation of the mechanics of the machine set up under the influence of the check and balance theory of government. The treaty-making power had been hard to fit into the general system, but finally had been intrusted to the executive and a part of the legislature. In the early exercise of this power each of these authorities was determined to assert to the full its constitutional rights. Yet each hesitated to exceed its authority lest it should find itself in active conflict with the other or with the House of Representatives. Thus political forces tended to keep each agent within the sphere of its legal competence, while at the same time, also as a matter of practical politics, each participated to some degree in performing a function which lay without that sphere. This interaction is inevitable in many phases of governmental activity, but in none, perhaps, is it more so than in the making of treaties which also are laws.

During the three years of negotiation which followed, the President, in his annual and special messages to Congress, continued to keep the Senate and the House equally informed of the progress of the negotiation. Whatever information he sent to the Senate he submitted also to the Representatives, a course which was in accord with the opinion of Jefferson, that when negotiating a treaty which would require subsequent legislation, it was good policy for the executive to keep in close touch with both branches of the legislature.[1]

The treaty, which was signed September 15, 1795, was transmitted to the Senate on the fifteenth of the following February, along with numerous papers and documents.[2] After three days of debate, the Senate referred it to a committee composed of Ellsworth, Cabot, King, Langdon, and Brown.[3] Their report estimated the expenditure required by the treaty as a sum considerably in excess of that previously authorized by the Senate, but at the same time recommended ratification.[4] Action was delayed for several days by Senators who apparently believed that the agreement to pay the sums stipulated in naval stores might lead to difficulties later. On March 2, however, ratification was advised by a very large majority, although a subsequent motion to change the form of the resolution by substituting "unanimously" for "two-thirds of the Senators present," failed, 16 to 11.[5]

It will be remembered that on February 22, 1791, the Senate had advised the President to secure

---

[1] *Am. State Papers, For. Rels.*, I. 288–300, 413–422.   Richardson *Messages*, I, 148, 152, 176–7.

[2] *Sen. Exec. Jour.*, I. 198; *Am. State Papers, For. Rels.*, I. 528–532.

[3] *Ibid.*, p. 199.   [4] *Ibid.*, pp. 200–201.

[5] *Sen. Exec. Jour.*, I. 201–202.

recognition of the treaty of 1787 with Morocco by the new Emperor of that state. Shortly afterwards an appropriation of $20,000 for this purpose was made by Congress.[1] Report of the progress of this negotiation was made to Congress in the message of December 16, 1793, concerning both the Moroccan and the Algerine questions. After the recognition of the treaty had been secured, however, it was to the Senate alone that a final report was made.[2]

THE TREATY OF SAN LORENZO EL REAL

Upon the third of March, 1796, the day following their final action on the treaty with Algiers, the Senate gave their advice and consent to the ratification of another convention which was of much greater importance to the nation. This was the treaty which had been signed at San Lorenzo el Real during the preceding October and which provided for the settlement of difficulties with Spain of thirteen years' standing. The chief points at issue concerned the boundary between the southern territory of the United States and West Florida, commerce between the two countries, and the navigation of the lower Mississippi by American citizens. Because it abandoned this latter right, or privilege, for a term of years the Jay-Gardoqui treaty, which was negotiated during the years 1785 and 1786, was rejected by the Congress of the

[1] *U. S. Statutes at Large*, I. 214 (Acts of 3d Sess. of 1st Cong., Stat. III, Ch. XVI).

[2] For a brief history of the Morocco Treaty, see Davis, *Notes Upon Foreign Treaties of the United States*, pp. 1242–1244.

Confederation. This body finally referred the entire matter to the new government under the Constitution.[1] By 1791 the situation had become such that the government practically faced the alternatives of securing the right to navigate the Mississippi to its mouth for citizens of the United States or of losing the allegiance of the settlers west of the Alleghenies and south of the Ohio. The relations between Spain and the powerful Indian tribes of the southwest increased the tension and it became "clear that an agreement or war must come. This was as plain to Spain as to Washington and his cabinet, and on December 16, 1791, the Spanish minister for foreign affairs made known the readiness of Madrid to negotiate."[2]

Early in January, 1792, the President sought the advice of the Senate in the matter, by laying before them a statement of the facts and asking conformation of the appointment of William Carmichael and William Short "to be Commissioners Plenipotentiary . . . for negotiating and concluding a convention, or treaty, concerning the navigation of

[1] Jay to Gardoqui, October 17, 1788. *Am. State Papers, For. Rels.*, I. 251.

[2] Chadwick, *The Relations of the United States and Spain: Diplomacy*, p. 35. Chapters I and II of this work briefly review the diplomatic relations between the two countries through the treaty of 1795. See also Rives, "Spain and the United States in 1795." *American Historical Review, IV. 62–79*, for the diplomacy leading up to the treaty, and particularly for an explanation of the reasons that led Spain to sign a convention so favorable to the United States. See also, Lyman, *Diplomacy of the United States*, I. vii, for account of Spanish American relations, 1777–1814; Moore, *International Law Digest*, V. 849–855; Bassett, *The Federalist System*, Ch. V.; Trescot, *The Diplomatic History of the Administrations of Washington and Adams*, 1789–1801, Ch. IV.

the river Mississippi by the citizens of the United
States; saving to the President and the Senate
their respective rights as to the ratification of the
same." [1]   After the Senate had confirmed these
nominations and thereby sanctioned the proposed
treaty, Spain expressed a desire to extend the
negotiations to cover all matters considered between Jay and Gardoqui in 1785 and 1786, particularly the commercial relations between the two
countries.   Jefferson believed that the Senate should
be consulted before the powers of the American
commissioners were extended to cover commercial
matters, and on March 7 the President laid before
it the proposed additional instructions.   In doing so
he definitely asked the Senate if they would "advise
and consent to the extension of the powers of the
Commissioners, as proposed, and to the ratification
of a treaty which shall conform to those instructions,
should they enter into such a one with that Court."
The message and the accompanying documents
were referred to a committee composed of Cabot,
Morris, and Langdon, and on the following day
the Secretary of the Treasury was asked to furnish
the Senate with detailed information concerning
the imports and exports of the states, individually,
for one year. [2]   On March 16 the Senate agreed to
the proposed extension of powers in a resolution
which is significant enough to be quoted in full.
It was as follows:

Resolved, (two-thirds of the Senators concurring therein,)
That they advise and consent to the extension of the
powers of the Commissioners as proposed, and that they

[1] *Sen. Exec. Jour.,* I. 95–96.   [2] *Ibid.,* pp. 106–110.

will advise and consent to the ratification of such treaty as the said Commissioners shall enter into with the Court of Spain, in conformity to those instructions.[1]

It should be noted that this resolution explicitly binds the Senate to agree to the ratification of a treaty concluded in conformity with the instructions which they had approved.

Two days after the Senate had consented to the extension of the scope of the negotiation, Jefferson submitted to Washington his instructions to the commissioners. These instructions deal with three subjects, — boundary, the navigation of the Mississippi, and commerce. Those given on the latter subject are verbatim as assented to by the Senate.[2] The instructions upon boundaries and the navigation of the Mississippi never had been laid before that body, however. This inconsistency in procedure shows to what extent Washington and the Senate transacted the business of treaty-making along the lines indicated by political convenience or necessity.

Spanish procrastination and "new combinations among the powers of Europe" having delayed the conclusion of the treaty for more than two years, Washington on November 21, 1794, nominated Thomas Pinckney, then Minister of the United States at the Court of St. James, as envoy extraordinary to conclude the negotiations. The terms in which Pinckney was nominated define his mission as identical with that with which Short and Carmichael had been charged, and later, in submitting

[1] Sen. Exec. Jour., I. 115.
[2] Am. State Papers, For. Rels., I. 252–257.

the treaty which he signed, the President informed the Senate that it had been negotiated under the original instructions to the earlier envoys, supplemented by a later instruction on the subject of spoliation claims.[1] On February 26, 1796, the Senate unanimously gave its advice and consent to the ratification of the treaty.[2]

[1] *Am. State Papers, For. Rels.*, I. 533; *Sen. Exec. Jour.*, I. 200.

[2] *Sen. Exec. Jour.*, I. 200, 201, 203.   A motion to "insert the word 'unanimously' instead of the words 'two-thirds of the Senators present,'" failed, 11 to 16.

CHAPTER IV

The Jay Treaty

WHILE the President and the Senate were working out the treaties thus far considered, they were also engaged, along with the House of Representatives, in the solution of the paramount problem of the early foreign affairs of the United States, that of our relations with Great Britain. The heritage of trouble arising out of the treaty of peace of 1783 which descended to the new federal government is too well understood to require discussion here, as are the subsequent events which finally presented to Washington's government the alternatives of concluding a treaty of some sort or of going to war with England.[1] The manner in which the Senate performed its part in Anglo-American affairs from 1790 to 1796, and the relations of the President with both Houses of Congress in the solution of the British problem are of primary importance, however, in the study of the exercise of the treaty-making powers of the Senate.

[1] Moore, *International Law Digest*, V. 699–707; Lyman, *Diplomacy of the United States*, I. xi., traces Anglo-American relations from 1783 through this treaty; Rankin, *The Treaty of Comity, Commerce and Navigation Between Great Britain and the United States, 1794*. Bassett, *The Federalist System*, Chs. IV, VIII; McMaster, *History of the People of the United States*, II. viii, xi; Foster, *A Century of American Diplomacy*, Ch. V; Trescot, *Diplomatic History*, Ch. II.

The question of British-American relations was first formally presented to the Senate on February 9, 1790, when Washington asked their advice as to the best method of settling the old dispute over the northeast boundary. The message states:

A plan for deciding this difference was laid before the late Congress; and whether that, or some other plan of a like kind, would not now be eligible, is submitted to your consideration.

In my opinion it is desirable that all questions between this and other nations should be speedily and amicably settled; and in this instance, I think it advisable to postpone any negotiations on the subject, until I shall be informed of the result of your deliberations, and receive your advice as to the propositions most proper to be offered on the part of the United States.

As I am taking measures for determining the intentions of Great Britain respecting the further detention of our posts,[1] etc., I am the more solicitous that the business now submitted to you may be prepared for negotiation, as soon as the other important affairs which engage your attention will permit.[2]

This message is characteristic of the early attitude of Washington towards the Senate as a council of advice in foreign affairs. It was referred, with the accompanying documents, to a committee composed of Strong, Butler, Patterson, Hawkins, and Johnson,[3] as was another communication on the subject subsequently received from Governor Hancock of Massachusetts.[4] Acting in accordance with the re-

---

[1] This refers to the mission of Gouverneur Morris.

[2] *Sen. Exec. Jour.*, I. 36–37; *Am. State Papers, For. Rels.*, I. 90–99.

[3] *Sen. Exec. Jour.*, I. 40.

[4] *Ibid.*, pp. 40–41; *Am. State Papers, For. Rels.*, I. 99.

port of this committee, the Senate advised that effectual measures should be taken to settle the dispute over the line. They suggested that the case first be presented to Great Britain, and that if other methods of amicable settlement failed, the disputes be referred to commissioners for decision in the manner advised by Jay in 1785 in the report which had been submitted to the Senate with the message of February 9.[1] The advice of the Senate seems to have been followed by no immediate action. It is interesting to note, however, that Article V of the Jay treaty provides for the decision of the St. Croix River boundary practically in the manner here recommended.

The mission of Gouverneur Morris, to which Washington had referred in his first message to the Senate, had disclosed the attitude of the British ministry towards the question at issue between the two countries. On February 14, 1791, the House was briefly informed that by informal conferences it had been ascertained that England was not disposed to enter into any arrangements merely commercial.[2] On the same day Washington put the Senate in full possession of the facts concerning Morris's mission, laying before them his instructions and reports.[3] Morris had been commissioned to prepare the way for a fulfillment of the treaty of 1783, to sound the ministry on the subject of a commercial convention, and to urge the sending of a British minister to the United States. The

---

[1] *Sen. Exec. Jour.*, I. 41–42.
[2] Richardson, *Messages*, I. 96.
[3] *Ibid.; Am. State Papers, For Rels.*, I. 121–127.

results of the mission were reported as being un-satisfactory with reference to the first two of its objects. Morris had been assured, however, that the government would send a diplomatic represen-tative to this country, and in October, 1791, George Hammond was received as minister from the Court of St. James.[1]

Hammond, however, had no authority to negotiate a settlement of any of the points at issue, and during the next three years the new republic and the ancient kingdom drifted steadily towards war. The old disputes were made more bitter by the addition of several grievances particularly galling to the United States. One of these grew out of the continued re-tention by the British of the border posts, which they now used as points of vantage from which to incite the Indians against the settlers in the western territory.[2] Friction arose from the destruction of American commerce and the impressment of Ameri-can seamen as an incident of the war between Great Britain and France. Then, too, many citizens, particularly among those who hated England and loved France, blamed the British for the renewed depredations of the Algerine pirates on our Mediter-ranean commerce. Public feeling was aroused to a pitch that is unknown in the United States to-day.

During this period Washington kept both houses of Congress well informed of developments. In February he laid before the legislature dispatches

---

[1] Foster, *A Century of American Diplomacy*, p. 159.

[2] See McLaughlin, "Western Posts and British Debts," in *American Historical Association Report*, 1894; also McLaughlin, *The Confederation and the Constitution*, Ch. VI.

from Pinckney which indicated that the British
government had small intention of hastening a
settlement. Correspondence between Randolph and
Hammond, likewise submitted, showed that no
progress had been made in the negotiations proposed
to be carried on at Philadelphia.[1] In the meantime Jefferson's long-expected commercial report
recommending reprisals against those European
nations which subjected American shipping to
harsh regulations had been laid before Congress.[2]
The House had responded by receiving favorably
Madison's resolutions proposing retaliatory measures
toward Great Britain.[3] At the same time the administration was preparing for eventualities by
proposing to provide for the fortification of harbors,
the increase of the navy, and the strengthening of
the army. The anti-English party in the country and
in Congress seemed to be preparing to meet Great
Britain more than halfway on the road to war.

Early in March it was realized that matters were
approaching a crisis. Washington's face was set
against war with England, however, and at this
juncture a small group of the most influential members of the Senate came forward with a plan once
more to substitute negotiations for hostilities.
The extent to which this group of Federalist Senators were responsible for the Jay treaty, the circumstances in which they worked to secure their
ends, and the manner in which Senate procedure

[1] *Am. State Papers, For. Rels.*, I. 327–328.

[2] *Annals of Congress*, 1793–1795, p. 152.

[3] These resolutions were introduced January 3, 1794. *Ibid.*,
p. 155 *et. seq.*

was adapted to meet their needs show that on the first occasion upon which the treaty-making power was the point of stress in a national crisis, it was exercised not in accordance with any *à priori* theory but as the necessities of the moment demanded. And the action of the Senate upon this treaty during the stages which preceded its signature, more closely approximates modern practice than does that taken upon any other treaty during the first decade of government under the Constitution.

Oliver Ellsworth of Connecticut, George Cabot and Caleb Strong of Massachusetts, and Rufus King of New York were the four Senators who, to a great extent, were responsible for the Jay mission. With them was associated Robert Morris of Pennsylvania. Federalists all, they were the backbone of the administration party in the Senate. Five more powerful men could not be selected from the Senators of that period. The fact that they were accustomed to working together and with Washington and his chief advisers made them an effective unit. Investigation reveals that they were more influential than any other members of the upper house in determining the action of that body in foreign affairs during the whole of Washington's administrations.

The time at which these men, or any of them, began to consider the possibility of a British mission has not been ascertained. There is reliable evidence, however, that early in March some such plan was well advanced.[1] By March 10 the project was so

[1] Brown, *Life of Oliver Ellsworth*, pp. 213–214. Here is given an excellent account of Ellsworth's activity in connection with the

well matured that the leaders in the movement met
in King's room to consider what action should be
taken in the emergency caused by the capture and
condemnation of American vessels in the West
Indies. What transpired at this meeting is best
told in the words of Rufus King himself. Under
date of March 10, he wrote:[1]

The order of Britain of the 6th Nov., authorizing the
seizing and sending in of American vessels for adjudica-
tion, having produced by the great number of captures
in the West Indies, the most alarming irritation in the
middle and eastern states (more than 200 sail having
been taken and nearly half that number having been
condemned), the faction opposed to the government
having taken hold of the circumstances to embarrass
and derange the administration — Ellsworth, Cabot and
Strong met at my room in order to confer on the course
most advisable to pursue.

The Result was that Ellsworth should go the next
day to the President, that he should represent to him
that the crisis was alarming; that war might and probably would be the consequence of these aggressions of
England, unless some system calculated to calm the public

Jay treaty. A detailed account of the genesis of the Jay mission is
given in Hamilton, *History of the Republic of the United States of
America*, V. cviii, civ. The author views the entire transaction
largely from Hamilton's viewpoint, but his statements are based on
contemporaneous sources, in part on the manuscript of Rufus
King, to which reference is made below. Reference also is made to
Lodge, *Life and Letters of George Cabot*, Chs. III, IV, where Cabot's
career in the Senate is traced; to an essay, "Oliver Ellsworth," by the
same author, in, *A Fighting Frigate and Other Essays and Addresses*,
pp. 86–89; and to Gibbs, *Memoirs of the Administrations of Washington and John Adams*, I. V. Here appears original material in
the form of letters to and from Oliver Wolcott.

[1] Rufus King's manuscript, a contemporary diary or record
written by King and published in Charles R. King, *Life and Correspondence of Rufus King*, I. 517–519.

mind, as well as the public councils, was speedily adopted
— to avoid that scourge and to save the national honor,
as well as to procure indemnification for the wrongs that
our merchants had already suffered. . . .

Ellsworth then was to suggest the adoption of
vigorous measures for defense, the sending of an
agent to the West Indies to report on the situation
there, and

that further an envoy extraordinary should be appointed
and sent to England to require satisfaction for the loss
of our Property and to adjust these points which menaced
a war between the two countries.

Hamilton was to be suggested as the man most
likely to succeed on such a mission.[1]

How Ellsworth fared with the President is recorded
in King's diary for March 12, as follows:

Ellsworth executed the mission agreed on upon the
10th instant. The President was at first reserved —
finally more communicative and apparently impressed
with Ellsworth's representation. Some doubts were
suggested respecting the character — that Col. Hamilton
did not possess the general confidence of the country —
that there could be no doubts in his, the President's
mind but that their existence was of some consequence.[2]

On this same day King "intimated to R. Morris
the purport of Ellsworth's mission to the President
— and proposed that he should, if occasion offered,
support it — he consented to do so." [3] Morris
kept his word and lent his powerful influence to
secure negotiation as a substitute for war. And
during the next month the proposition advanced

[1] *Life and Correspondence of Rufus King*, I. 517–519.
[2] *Ibid.*   [3] *Ibid.*

by Ellsworth and his colleagues needed all the support that it could command. The whole project of a mission was bitterly assailed by all Republicans and many Federalists. Furthermore, Washington had unerringly divined the weakness of Hamilton in the rôle of envoy to England. The proposal to nominate him raised such a storm of protest that finally it became evident that from a political standpoint, his appointment was impossible. On April 8 Washington told Morris that he had thought of the Vice-President, Hamilton, Jay and Jefferson for the task.[1] The attitude of the five Senators seems to have been, Hamilton if possible, if not, then Jay.[2] Together with Hamilton they finally acquiesced in the selection of the Chief Justice, and

[1] *Life and Correspondence of Rufus King*, I., p. 519.

[2] "Ap. 12. Mr. Jay arrived to hold a circuit Court in Phila. — he came to my room, the conversation soon turned to the present situation of the Country. I told him that the object of the Friends of peace was such as was agreed between Ellsworth, Cabot, Strong and myself on the 10. Mar.; that I had heard from the Pr. had mentioned the Vice President, Hamilton, Jefferson and him as persons whom he had thought of for the Envoyship; that his friends were decided that it must be him or Hamilton.

"That so far as regarded the particular knowledge of the Cabinet, and the details of Commerce, Hamilton might deserve a preference. But that in other respects we should be perfectly satisfied with him; that these points were not very important, and if on the other hand, we consider weight of character abroad as well as at home, his appointment might be more advantageous than that of Hamilton. Besides that Hamilton was essential in his present station. Mr. Jay gave no Reply respecting himself but appeared fully to agree in the Propriety of Hamilton's appointment.

"We conversed respecting the Resolution before the House for cutting off commercial intercourse and sequestering British Debts. He joined me in opinion that they would frustrate all negotiations and said he should tell the President so when he saw him." *Ibid.*

on the fourteenth, Hamilton addressed a long letter
to Washington urging the necessity of the mission,
setting forth the dangerous character of the House
propositions for commercial and other reprisals,
withdrawing his name from consideration, and urging the appointment of Jay.[1]   Thus it was decided
that Jay should be the envoy.   King records that
on April 15 Hamilton, Strong, Cabot, Ellsworth,
and himself waited upon the Chief Justice to urge
his acceptance of the post.[2]   That night in a very
grave letter Jay informed his wife that there was
"here a serious determination to send me to England,
if possible to avert a war."   And he declared that
if on investigation he should be convinced that it
was his duty to go he would accept the appointment.[3]

[1] *The Works of Alexander Hamilton*, V. 97–115; also, Hamilton
History of the Republic, V. 544–554

[2] King wrote, "Hamilton, Strong, Cabot, Ellsworth and myself
went to Mr. Jay this afternoon to press upon him the necessity
which exists that he should not decline the Envoyship; that in
short he was the only man in whom we could confide, and that we
deemed the situation of the Country too interesting and critical
to permit him to hesitate.

"He did not decline.   We urged the idea that he should reinforce
the opinion that the measures before the House wd. disappoint the
objects sought for in the appointment — and that he could not
consent to be Envoy charged with complaint and menace." *Life
and Correspondence of Rufus King*, I. 520.

[3] The gravity of the situation at this time is strikingly shown
by two letters from John Jay to his wife.   On April 9 he wrote:
"I arrived here on Monday evening, and yesterday dined with the
President.   The question of war or peace seems to be as much in
suspension here as in New York when I left you.   I am rather
inclined to think that peace will continue, but should not be sur-
prised if war should take place.   In the present state of things, it will
be best to be ready for the *latter* event in *every* respect."

And on April 10: "The aspect of the times is such, that prudential
arrangements calculated on the prospect of war should not be

Consideration over night evidently convinced him that he should do so, for on the following day Oliver Ellsworth wrote to his friend Oliver Wolcott, saying that Jay had just informed him of his determination to accept the appointment if it should be made.[1]

In the meantime Washington had decided upon his course of action. On the evening of the fourteenth he had requested Randolph to draw up a message to submit the plan and the nomination to the Senate. Early the following morning he asked if the document would be ready by 11 o'clock in order that it might be laid before "the gentlemen with whom I usually advise on these occasions." [2]   Twenty-four

neglected, nor too long postponed. Peace or war appears to me a question which cannot be solved. . . . There is much irritation and agitation in this town, and in Congress. Great Britain has acted unwisely and unjustly; and there is some danger of our acting intemperately." *Correspondence and Public Papers of John Jay*, IV. 2, 3.

[1] Ellsworth to Oliver Wolcott, April 16, 1794. Gibbs, *Memoirs of the Administrations of Washington and Adams*, I. 135.

[2] Washington-Randolph, April 15, 1794, *Washington's Writings* XII. 419. It is interesting to note that at this moment Washington was considering laying before the Senate the outline of the entire plan of action which he thought it would become necessary to follow should the Jay mission fail. Continuing in his letter to Randolph, he said: "My objects are, to prevent a war, if justice can be obtained by fair and strong representations (to be made by a special envoy) of the injuries which this country has sustained from Great Britain in various ways, to put it in a complete state of military defence, and to provide *eventually* for such measures as seem now to be pending in Congress for execution, if negotiation in a reasonable time proves unsuccessful.

"Such is the train of my thoughts; but how far all, or any of them, except the first, ought to be introduced into the message, in the present stage of the business in Congress, deserves, as I have said before, due consideration." The message sent in on the day

hours later, April 16, 1794, the message nominating Jay as Envoy Extraordinary of the United States to his Britannic Majesty was sent to the Senate.[1] The President had done his part towards carrying out the plan suggested by the five Senators. It now remained for them to secure the consent of their colleagues to the mission. This proved to be a task as interesting as it was difficult.

The minority in the Senate based their opposition to confirmation upon three grounds. They maintained: first, that it was unnecessary and inexpedient to dispatch an envoy extraordinary to carry on a negotiation that could be as well or better conducted by Thomas Pinckney, Minister of the United States at London; second, that the Chief Justice of the United States should not be

following was limited to the subject of negotiation and the nomination of Jay as envoy. *Ibid.*

[1] The Message was as follows: *"Gentlemen of the Senate:* The communications which I have made to you during your present session, from the despatches of our Minister in London, contain a serious aspect of our affairs with Great Britain. But as peace ought to be pursued with unremitted zeal, before the last resource, which has so often been the scourge of nations, and cannot fail to check the advanced prosperity of the United States, is contemplated; I have thought proper to nominate, and do hereby nominate, John Jay, as Envoy Extraordinary of the United States, to his Britannic Majesty.

"My confidence in our Minister Plenipotentiary at London, continues undiminished. But a mission like this, while it corresponds with the solemnity of the occasion, will announce to the world the solicitude for a friendly adjustment of our complaints, and a reluctance to hostility. Going immediately from the United States, such an Envoy will carry with him a full knowledge of the existing temper and sensibilities of our country, and will thus be taught to vindicate our rights with firmness, and to cultivate peace with sincerity." *Sen. Exec. Jour.,* I. 150.

sent to negotiate a treaty which might later come before him for judicial consideration;[1] third, that John Jay held opinions against the interest and just claims of his country which rendered it unwise to entrust to him the task of securing justice from Great Britain.[2] Thus the Senate debated and passed not only upon the choice of the envoy but also upon the expediency of the mission itself.

It did not, however, have an opportunity either to approve or to disapprove of the proposals which Jay was to make to England, although the precedents might have led it to expect that his instructions would be laid before it. On April 16 King wrote, "From the difficulty of passing particular instructions in the Senate, it seems to me the most suitable that the Pr. shd. instruct, and that the

[1] The final attempt to prevent or delay the confirmation of Jay's nomination was made by the introduction of a motion by Burr to postpone its consideration for the purpose of considering the following:

"*Resolved*, That any communications to be made to the Court of Great Britain may be made through our Minister now at that Court, with an equal facility and effect, and at much less expense, than by an Envoy Extraordinary; and that such an appointment is at present inexpedient and unnecessary.

"That to permit Judges of the Supreme Court to hold at the same time any other office or employment, emanating from and holden at the pleasure of the Executive, is contrary to the spirit of the Constitution, and, as tending to expose them to the influence of the Executive is mischievous and impolitic." This motion failed 10 to 17. *Sen. Exec. Jour.*, I. 152. Also *Life and Correspondence of Rufus King*, I. 522.

[2] *Life and Correspondence of Rufus King*, I. 521; *Sen. Exec. Jour.*, I. 150–153; Hamilton, *History of the Republic*, V. cv., Trescot, *Diplomatic History of the Administrations of Washington and Adams*, pp. 101–105, gives an excellent discussion of the objections raised to the choice of Jay for this mission.

Treaty shd. be concluded subject to the approbation of the Senate."[1] Federalist leaders were not
unprepared then when, on the day following, a
motion was introduced,

That previous to going into the nomination of a special
Envoy to the Court of Great Britain, the President of
the United States be requested to inform the Senate of
the whole business with which the proposed Envoy is
to be charged.

They promptly secured the rejection of the proposition.[2]

The feeling which then existed both in and out
of Congress was such that the "difficulty of passing
particular instructions in the Senate" certainly
would have been great. Indeed it is unlikely that
the Senate could have been brought to agree to any
detailed plan that Washington and his advisers
might have submitted. In these circumstances it
was evidently recognized that if the Senate was
to serve as a "council of advice" in such a delicate
matter it must be through a small number of its
members in whom both the executive and a majority
of their colleagues had great confidence. In later
years this became the normal mode of procedure.
The significance of the precedent set in this instance
will be discussed more fully in connection with the
ratification of the treaty.

After three days of discussion Jay's nomination
was confirmed.[3] The minority attempted without
success to obtain the passage of a resolution that in
executive business the minority on any question

---

[1] *Life and Correspondence of Rufus King*, I. 521.
[2] *Sen. Exec. Jour.*, I. 151.   [3] *Ibid.*, I. 152.

might enter their objections in the journals.[1] It will be remembered that a similar resolution introduced at the time of the confirmation of the Creek treaty of 1790 failed.[2]

It now remained to instruct the envoy and to dispatch him to England. In this phase of the business the Senatorial group still exercised a powerful if not a predominant influence. King's diary records under date of April 21 that Hamilton, Ellsworth, Cabot, and he met with Jay to discuss the subject.

All agreed that as the Pr. might give the instructions without consulting the Senate, it would be most advisable so to conduct the business, and that the Treaty, if any shd. be formed, should be signed subject to the approbation of the Senate.[3]

The question of spoliations on American commerce and that of the execution of the old treaty were considered, as, indeed, was the entire field of the proposed negotiation. In King's words,

V.arious propositions relative to a commercial Treaty, the posts, the Indian trade, the navigation of the Lakes, the West Indies, etc., etc., were also discussed — and Mr. —— stated his conversation with the Secretary of State who appeared disposed to leave the negotiation open and the powers of the envoy very discretionary.[3]

---

[1] *Sen. Exec. Jour.*, I. 152, 153.   [2] See p. 29 above.

[3] *Life and Correspondence of Rufus King*, I. 523.

This general principle was the one acted upon by Randolph in framing the instructions, part VI. of which contains the following words: You will therefore consider the ideas, herein expressed, as amounting to recommendations only, which in your discretion you may modify, as seems most beneficial to the United States, except in the two following cases, which are immutable." Then follow references to his instructions on the relations of the United States

It is not unlikely that other informal conferences were held between the leaders of the Senate and executive officials before the instructions which Randolph handed to Jay, May 6, were finally completed. Hamilton himself had a large part in drafting the instructions, and before Jay's departure submitted his views to him very fully in a long letter covering many of the most important problems to be solved.[1] The entire procedure, certainly, is very similar to that by which it later became customary to consult the Senate through the Committee on Foreign Relations before any important negotiation was embarked upon.[2]

to France, and on a commercial treaty. *Am. State Papers, For. Rels.*, I. 474.

Hamilton's low opinion of these instructions and the degree to which the senatorial group depended upon the inclination and ability of Jay to carry out the measures upon which they had agreed is strikingly exhibited by the following paragraph in a letter written to Washington after the signature of the treaty: "I mentioned as my opinion that the instructions to Mr. Jay, if published, would do harm. The truth, unfortunately, is that it is in general a crude mass, which will do no credit to the administration. This was my impression of it at the time, but the delicacy of attempting too much reformation in the work of another head of department, the hurry of the moment; and a great confidence in the person sent, prevented my attempting that reformation. Hamilton to Washington, March 28, 1796. *Works of Alexander Hamilton*, X. 152–153.

As a member of the cabinet, however, Hamilton had a part in drawing up these instructions, submitting memorandums of points to be included in them, and partial drafts upon the commercial sections to Washington and Randolph. Hamilton to Washington, April 23, 1794; Hamilton to Randolph, April 27, 1794; Draft of part of instructions to Jay. *Ibid.*, V. 115–123; See also, Hamilton, *History of the Republic*, VI. cxvii.

[1] Hamilton to Jay, May 6, 1794. *Works of Alexander Hamilton*, V. 123–128.

[2] It is pointed out by William Garrott Brown that on November 19, the day upon which the treaty was signed besides letters to

It was in April, 1794, that the Senate finally confirmed the nomination of the special envoy. Eleven months later, on the seventh of March, 1795, the Jay treaty was placed in the hands of the President.[1] Congress had adjourned four days previously. But before the Senators had left Philadelphia Washington had issued a proclamation requesting them to assemble in special session on June 8.[2] Upon the appointed day he was informed that the Senate was ready to receive any communications he might care to make, the treaty was transmitted, and the fight for ratification was on.

It is not considered to be within the scope of this study to trace in detail the political struggle over the Jay treaty either in ·Congress or out of it. It is deemed important, however, to outline the most significant steps in the procedure by which the Senate finally advised and consented to ratification with the condition that the twelfth article be suspended; to estimate the degree to which the dominant group of Federalist statesmen were responsible

Washington and Edmund Randolph, Secretary of State, Jay wrote to Hamilton, King, and Ellsworth, making a kind of brief report to each. Brown, *Life of Oliver Ellsworth, 217*. *Correspondence and Public Papers of Jay*, IV. 132–149.

[1] McMaster, *History of the People*, II. 213.

[2] Richardson, *Messages*, I. 587. Several months later in a letter to Monroe relating what had occurred Madison states, "The Treaty concluded by him did not arrive until a few days after the 3rd. of March which put an end to the last session of Congress. . . . According to previous notification to the Senators that branch assembled on the 28th (in) of June, the contents of the Treaty being in the meantime impenetrably concealed. I understand it was even withheld from the Secretaries of War and the Treasury, that is Pickering and Wolcott." Madison to Monroe, December 20 1795, *Writings of James Madison* (Hunt edition), VI. 257–258.

for this action; to examine the methods by which Burr and his associates opposed ratification; and to observe the manner in which the Senate attempted to guard the secrecy of its proceedings.

The first move of the opponents of ratification was an attempt to secure the publication of the treaty and the instructions under which it had been negotiated. For five days after June 8 the contest was over this question.[1] On the thirteenth the Republicans abandoned this line of attack and the debate was turned to the provisions of the treaty itself.[2] It soon became evident that the twelfth article was the vulnerable point in the product of Jay's endeavors, and on the sixteenth it was agreed that it should not be taken up until the rest of the treaty had been discussed.[3]

It is significant that the proposition to amend the treaty by the addition of an article suspending so much of this twelfth article as related to the trade between the United States and the British West Indies originated not from the enemies of the treaty but from its friends. It is hardly accurate to say that the opposition Senators succeeded in striking out this article.[4] In fact, the suggestion that the Senate advise ratification with this condition seems to have come from the very group that was so largely responsible for the mission itself. Before the Senate had convened, Hamilton had written to William Bradford, Senator from Rhode Island, telling him that the commercial agreement in the treaty displeased him and declaring that he

---

[1] See pp. 88–91 *below.* [2] *Sen. Exec. Jour.*, I. 181–182.
[3] *Ibid.*, I. 182. [4] Brown, *Life of Oliver Ellsworth*, p. 218.

preferred a conditional ratification to an unqualified acceptance of the instrument.[1] Three days after the debate had commenced Hamilton also wrote to Rufus King advising the same course.[2] On June 17 a resolution was introduced giving the advice and consent of the Senate to ratification,

on condition that there shall be added to the said treaty an article whereby it shall be agreed to suspend the operation of so much of the 12th article as respects the trade which his said Majesty thereby consents may be carried on between the United States and his islands in the West Indies in the manner, and on the terms and conditions therein specified.

And the Senate recommend to the President, to proceed without delay, to further friendly negotiations with his Majesty, on the subject of the said trade, and of the terms and conditions in question.[3]

This resolution is said to have been introduced by King himself.[4] Considering the care with which he and his friends controlled every step towards the consummation of their end, this was probably the case. At any rate it formulated the course which they had determined to follow.

After the seventeenth two major moves were made to prevent ratification, and in addition there was one serious attempt to couple with the recommendation of further negotiations on the West India trade

---

[1] *Works of Alexander Hamilton*, X. 99.

[2] *Ibid.*, p. 101. See Hamilton, *History of the Republic*, VI. cxviii, for discussion of Hamilton's part in securing the ratification of the treaty.

[3] *Sen. Exec. Jour.*, I. 182.

[4] King, *Life and Correspondence of Rufus King*, II. 9–10. The author makes this statement in guarded form, and gives no evidence to substantiate it.

a similar recommendation with reference to compensation for negroes or other American property carried away in violation of Article VII of the treaty of peace.[1] While the way was being prepared for these propositions the President at the request of the Senate sent in various documents bearing upon the treaty.[2]

On the twenty-second Burr introduced the motion upon which the real trial of strength between the parties was to be made. This motion may be considered to express the opinion of at least a large number of Senators as to the lengths to which it was proper for the Senate to go in advising the President to secure specific amendments to a treaty by means of new negotiations. Burr moved the following resolution:

That the further consideration of the treaty concluded at London, the 19th of November, 1794, be postponed, and that it be recommended to the President of the United States, to proceed without delay to further friendly negotiations with his Britannic Majesty, in order to effect alterations in the said treaty, in the following particulars:

Then followed seven propositions involving the amendment or excision of ten articles in the treaty as signed.[3] The alterations requested represented

[1] *Sen. Exec. Jour.*, I. 183.   [2] *Ibid.*

[3] The alterations recommended were as follows:

"That the 9th, 10th, and 24th articles, and so much of the 25th as relates to the shelter of refuge to be given to the armed vessels of States or Sovereigns at war with either party be expunged.

2d art. That no privilege or right be allowed to the settlers or traders mentioned in the 2d article, other than those which are secured to them by the treaty of 1783, and existing laws.

3d art. That the third article be expunged, or be so modified that the citizens of the United States may have the use of *all* rivers,

the demands of the anti-administration, anti-British party. So far as their practicability was concerned, the President might as well have been advised to secure the cession of Canada to the United States. Nevertheless they were supported by the ten Senators who acted together in every attack upon the treaty. The vote against the adoption of the resolution was 20 to 10.[1]

But although Burr's proposal was defeated there is nothing to indicate that the rejection was not based purely upon expediency and not at all upon the impropriety of the recommendation that the President make a new treaty in accordance with the ideas of the Senate. In fact, a resolution of

ports and places within the territories of His Britannic Majesty in North America, in the same manner as his subjects may have those of the United States.

"6th art. That the value of the negroes and other property carried away, contrary to the 7th article of the treaty of 1783, *and the loss and damage sustained to the United States by the detention of the posts,* be paid for by the British government; the amount to be ascertained by the Commissioners who may be appointed to liquidate the claims of the British creditors.

"12th art. That what relates to the West India trade, and the provisions and conditions thereof, of the 12th article, be expunged, or be rendered more favorable to the United States, and without any restraint on the exportation, in vessels of the United States, of any articles, not the growth, produce, or manufacture of the said islands of his Britannic Majesty.

"15th art. That no clause be admitted which may restrain the United States from reciprocating benefits by discriminating between foreign nations in their commercial arrangements, or prevent them from increasing the tonnage or other duties on British vessels, on terms of reciprocity, or in stipulated ratio.

"21st art. That the subjects of citizens of either party, be not restrained from accepting commissions in the army or navy of any foreign power." *Sen. Exec. Jour.,* I. 183–184.

[1] *Sen. Exec. Jour.,* I. 184.

similar form had been passed in 1793 in connection with General Putnam's treaty with the Wabash and Illinois Indians.[1] The Senate had not been formally consulted as to the instructions under which Jay acted. It had been so consulted prior to the negotiation of other treaties — had been treated as a "council" whose advice ought to be sought before a treaty was negotiated. Taking these facts into consideration, Burr's resolution was in full accord with the accepted theory of the position of the Senate in treaty-making. So far as a treaty with Great Britain was concerned the adoption of such a resolution would have made a treaty impossible, which of course is the political reason which caused the Federalists to reject the proposal.

It is probable that the passage of this resolution would have modified the subsequent development and exercise of the treaty-making powers of the Senate. Washington might well have considered such an act as notice that, in the future, the Senate would expect to participate in the determination of the conditions under which a proposed treaty would be signed; at the very least it would have suggested forcibly the expediency of always consulting them before opening negotiations. It might also have led the Senate to expect such consultation and thus have made it easier for Senators or groups of Senators to demand it. A legislative body eagerly creates and tenaciously clings to precedents which increase its power and enhance its dignity and importance. At the time Jay's nomination was before them, however, the necessities of the situation and the

[1] See above, p. 35.

political influence of the Federalist leaders were powerful enough to keep the Senate from demanding the instructions which were to be issued to him. The same forces were now sufficient to lead the Senate to waive for the good of the nation and of the Federalist party what it might well have regarded as its established prerogatives. Thus the precedent which was established weakened rather than strengthened its position in treaty-making. The first great treaty under the Constitution had been negotiated by the executive alone. Not until the signed agreement was laid before it had the Senate been formally consulted as to its terms. A determined attempt to prevent ratification until new negotiations had been attempted along lines laid down by the Senate had failed. The course adopted by Washington in shifting his relations with the Senate in this matter from a basis of theory to one of expediency had been justified by events and accepted by the Senate.

On June 24, the day following the rejection of Burr's proposal, an attempt was made to add to the resolution of advice and consent, the recommendation that the President continue negotiations for the purpose of securing adequate compensation for negroes carried off by the British in contravention of the treaty of peace. The motion to this effect was presented by Jacob Read, Federalist Senator from South Carolina, and was seconded by Pierce Butler, his Republican colleague.[1] It was lost by a vote of 12 to 15, Read himself and Humphrey Marshall of Kentucky moving from the Federalist

[1] *Sen. Exec. Jour.*, I. 185.

phalanx to vote for the interests of the slave owners.
It is interesting to note the sectional character of
this division, every southern Senator except Gunn
of Georgia voting for the amendment, while Burr,
Langdon of New Hampshire, and Robinson of
Vermont cast the only northern votes in favor of
the proposal.[1] The subsequent fate of this proposition may be mentioned here. On June 25, after
the Senate had advised the ratification of the treaty,
James Gunn, the Federalist Senator from Georgia,
introduced a resolution advising further negotiation
to obtain compensation for the slaveholders and
suggesting that in case this should fail the President
attempt to secure an agreement to submit the claims
to a joint commission. Coupled with it was a paragraph declaring the opinion of the Senate to be that
the negotiation on this subject should be distinct
from and subsequent to that recommended in their
resolution of the twenty-fourth respecting the West
India trade. The Republicans refused to accept the
resolution with this declaration, and as Henry of
Maryland was not in the chamber when the final
vote came, the Federalists lacked one of the twenty
votes necessary to secure its passage.[2]

After this attempt to care for the interests of the
slaveholders had failed, the minority made their
final stand. A resolution was introduced that the
President be informed that the Senate would not
consent to the ratification of the treaty for seven
different reasons which were set forth in detail.[3]

---

[1] *Sen. Exec. Jour.*, I. 185. [2] *Ibid.*, pp. 187–189.
[3] The following reasons were stated:
"1st. Because so much of the treaty as was intended to ter-

The object of this resolution probably was to write into the record a final and formal statement of the grounds upon which the minority opposed the treaty. It was promptly voted down.

The Federalists then exerted their power and forced their resolution of the seventeenth to a vote. The question was divided and that part of the resolu-

minate the complaints flowing from the inexecution of the treaty of 1783, contains stipulations that were not rightfully or justly requirable of the United States, and which are both impolitic and injurious to their interests; and because the treaty hath not secured that satisfaction from the British government, for the removal of negroes in violation of the treaty of 1783, to which the citizens of the United States were justly entitled.

"2nd. Because the rights of individual states are, by the ninth article of the treaty, unconstitutionally invaded.

"3d. Because, however impolitic or unjust it may generally be to exercise the power prohibited by the tenth article, yet it rests on legislative discretion, and ought not to be prohibited by treaty.

"4th. Because so much of the treaty as relates to commercial arrangements between the parties, wants that reciprocity upon which alone such like arrangements ought to be founded, and will operate ruinously to the American commerce and navigation.

"5th. Because the treaty prevents the United States from the exercise of that control over their commerce and navigation, as connected with other nations, which might better the condition of their intercourse with friendly nations.

"6th. Because the treaty asserts a power in the President and Senate, to control, and even annihilate the constitutional right of the Congress of the United States over their commercial intercourse with foreign nations.

"7th. Because, if the construction of this treaty should not produce an infraction of the treaties now subsisting between the United States and their allies, it is calculated to excite sensations which may not operate beneficially to the United States.

"Notwithstanding the Senate will not consent to the ratification of this treaty, they advise the President of the United States to continue his endeavors, by friendly negotiation with his Britannic Majesty, to adjust all the real causes of complaint between the two nations." *Sen. Exec. Jour.*, I. 185–186.

tion advising and consenting to ratification, provided that the twelfth article be amended, was carried by the party vote of 20 to 10. The remaining paragraph, advising further negotiation on the West India trade was then unanimously agreed to.[1] Thus the result of Washington's final effort to avert the "scourge of nations" was accepted by the Senate with only such modifications as were suggested by the leaders of the Federalist party and likely to be agreed to by Great Britain.

The assent of the Senate to conditional ratification at once gave rise to the question of the proper procedure to be followed in making the proposed additional article a part of the treaty. Republican Senators declared that the entire treaty would have to be resubmitted to the Senate before ratification.[2] On June 29 the President submitted a copy of the Senate resolution to the Secretaries of State, Treasury, and War, and to the Attorney General, together with these two questions:

First, is or is not that resolution intended to be the final act of the Senate; or do they expect, that the new article which is proposed shall be submitted to them before the treaty takes effect?

Secondly, does or does not the constitution permit the President to ratify the treaty, without submitting the new article, after it shall be agreed to by the British King, to the Senate for their further advice and consent?[3]

[1] *Sen. Exec. Jour.*, I. 186.

[2] Crandall, *Treaties, Their Making and Enforcement* (2d ed.) p. 81, citing Tazewell to Monroe, June 27, 1795, MS. Monroe Papers, VIII. 951.

[3] Written about June 29, 1795, *Washington's Writings*, XIII, 59, 60.

The Secretaries and the Attorney General were
agreed in the opinion that it was unnecessary to
submit the new article to the Senate.[1] Hamilton,
upon this first consideration of the question at least,
seems to have taken the other position. Accustomed to rely upon his assistance in weighty
matters, Washington had requested his advice upon
the ratification of the treaty even though he was no
longer in official position;[2] and in particular had
asked his opinion as to the proper course to be
pursued on this point.[3] Washington, seriously considered Hamilton's advice and as he was leaving
Philadelphia for Mt. Vernon on July 14, he requested his former Secretary of the Treasury to
lay his ideas before Randolph, if, upon mature re-
flection, he should continue to disagree with the
position taken by the latter and his colleagues.
He also informed Randolph of Hamilton's opinion
and asked him to discuss the subject again with
the other officers of the government.[4] There is no
record that Hamilton further expressed his views
on this matter either to Washington or to Randolph.
Possibly he realized that a resubmission would have
jeopardized the entire treaty and for this reason
decided to hold his peace. That the opponents of

[1] Washington to Hamilton, July 14, 1795, *Ibid.*, p. 67.

[2] Hamilton's resignation was accepted January 31, 1793.
McMaster, *History of the People*, II. 212.

[3] Washington to Hamilton, July 3, 1795, *Washington's Writings*
XIII. 61–63; Washington to Hamilton, July 13, 1795, *Ibid.*, pp.
63–67.

[4] Washington to Hamilton, July 14, 1795, *Washington's Writings*, XIII. 67.

the administration felt that they had nothing to lose and everything to gain by resubmission, explains their position upon the constitutional point. Jefferson, for example, in writing to Tazewell, observed:

I am not without hope that the operations of the 12th article may render a recurrence to the Senate yet necessary, and so give to the majority an opportunity of correcting the error into which their exclusion of public light has led them.[1]

Whatever may have been Hamilton's ultimate opinion, Washington finally acted upon the advice of the heads of the departments, and the course then laid out has been uniformly followed since when the Senate has advised and consented to the ratification of treaties under certain conditions, usually in the form of definite amendments. Randolph admirably expressed the principle upon which this action is based.

The Secretary of State, in his written opinion, on July 12, argued that, as the final ratification was given by the President, and not by the Senate, the action of the Senate, even in case it advised and consented unconditionally, was taken upon a treaty the completion of which was reserved to the President; that the Senate consequently might give its advice and consent without having the very treaty which was to be ratified before it; that if the President should ratify without again consulting that body, he would be responsible for the accuracy with which its advice was followed; and that if he should ratify what had not been advised, the treaty, for that very reason, would not be the supreme law of the land, and in this lay the security of the Senate.[2]

[1] Jefferson to Tazewell, September 13, 1795, *Writings of Thomas Jefferson*, IX. 308.

[2] Crandall, *Treaties, Their Making and Enforcement* (2d ed.), pp. 80–81. Reference to *MS*. Washington Papers, XXII. 148, 184, 200.

The decision thus made was of vital importance. Had it been decided that resubmission to the Senate in such circumstances was necessary and that when resubmitted a treaty was again liable to rejection or amendment, the power of the Senate would have been appreciably increased and our system of ratification made even more complicated.

By August 14 Washington finally had made his decision that he would follow the advice of the Senate and attempt to secure England's ratification of the treaty with the twelfth article amended.[1] This he had no difficulty in doing. Even though the business of exchange finally fell into the hands of W. A. Deas, who as American chargé in the absence of Thomas Pinckney seems to have made himself unpopular at the British Foreign Office. Lord Grenville raised no objection whatever to the inclusion of an additional article as required by the resolution of the Senate.[2] Inasmuch as later British foreign ministers protested with more asperity than courtesy against the American custom of ratifying treaties conditionally or with amendments proposed by the Senate, the position taken by Lord Grenville upon this occasion is worthy of exposition.[3]

In his report of a conference with Grenville on the morning of the twenty-third, Deas informed Pinckney that upon stating that he

[1] Randolph to Adams, August 14, 1795, *MS.* State Department, U. S. Ministers, Instructions, III. 24.

[2] *Memoirs of John Quincy Adams*, I. 122.

[3] Much of the correspondence referred to in this discussion is to be found in Trescot, *The Diplomatic History of the Administrations of Washington and Adams*, pp. 119–120.

was possessed of the President's Ratification of the Treaty conformably to the Advice of the Senate and offering to exchange the same for an equivalent Ratification on the part of this Government, his Lordship observed *unofficially* that he had no reason to think such exchange would not take place, but that it would be necessary to lay the business before the King for his Determination.[1]

Five days later Deas was able to announce the exchange of ratifications. It is evident that Great Britain at this time expressed no disapproval whatever at the modification by the Senate of the treaty as signed, for Deas wrote to Pickering that

Lord Grenville in presenting that [the ratification] on the part of their Government expressed the satisfaction it afforded the King in giving his assent. You will observe from the copy of the British Ratification herein enclosed that it corresponds with that of the President.[2]

---

[1] William A. Deas to Secretary of State, October 23, 1795, *MS*. State Department, England, Vol. III.

[2] William A. Deas to Secretary of State, October 28, 1795, *Ibid.*

It may be observed that the long delay in the promulgation of the Jay treaty probably was due to the fact that Deas forwarded to the State Department only a copy of the British ratification instead of the original. His letter of October 28, announcing the exchange of ratifications, is endorsed as having been received at the Department on December 28. Two months more passed before the treaty was proclaimed, during which time the Republicans roundly abused Washington for his silence on the subject. McMaster, *History of the People*, II. 263. A letter from Pickering to Deas dated March 9, 1796, explains the delay as follows: "No original ratification having arrived, as expected the President at length directed the treaty with Great Britain to be promulgated, on the evidence of its ratification by his Majesty contained in your letter of October 28th. But the daily expectation of an *original*, induced the suspension of this promulgation until the 29th of February, and the next day the treaty was laid before each House of Congress." Pickering to Deas, March 9, 1796. *MS*. State Department, United States Ministers, Vol. III.

On February 29, 1796, the President proclaimed
the treaty without further consultation with the Senate upon the form of ratification, and on March 1
laid it before both Houses of Congress.[1] The propriety and constitutionality of this course seems to
have been unquestioned at the time. Certainly
there is no record of any protest from the Senate
or from individual Senators.

In the matter of propriety, in fact, the Senate
had been put in no pleasant position by the action
of one of its own members. When Washington
had transmitted the treaty and the documents connected with it his message had been silent upon the
subject of secrecy. Neither the treaty itself nor
the documents were submitted "in confidence."
The question at once arose, however, whether the
Senate should regard the matter as confidential,
and during the very first session an order was passed
laying the Senators under an injunction of secrecy
concerning the communications received from the
President.[2] It was further directed that thirty-one
copies of the treaty be printed, under injunction of
secrecy, for the use of the Senate. On the following
day two additional copies were authorized.[3] On the
twelfth, the opponents of ratification made a determined effort to secure the publication of the treaty.
But on the thirteenth the motion to rescind the resolution enjoining secrecy was defeated by the strict
party vote that had marked the divisions on all of
the important phases of the struggle for ratification.[4]

---

[1] *Annals of Congress*, 1795–1796, pp. 48, 394.
[2] *Sen. Exec. Jour.*, I. 178.   [3] *Ibid*.
[4] *Ibid.*, pp. 178, 179, 181.

Thus the matter stood until after the final action of the Senate on the treaty.

On June 25 the matter was again brought up by Burr, who moved that the resolution of the eighth enjoining secrecy upon the Senators be rescinded, but that they nevertheless be enjoined not to authorize or allow any publication in print of the treaty or any article thereof. Ellsworth endeavored, unsuccessfully, to substitute for this an order that until ratification the question of publication should be left solely with the President. Burr's motion was then adopted as presented but was at once reconsidered. On the next day, however, after much debate and several divisions a resolution was carried removing the injunction of secrecy but forbidding the Senators to give out any copy of the treaty or of any article thereof.[1]

The action of the Senate in refusing to authorize the publication of the treaty or any article thereof seems to have come from a feeling among a majority

---

[1] *Sen. Exec. Jour.*, I. 190, 191, 192. With reference to this action Madison wrote to Monroe, December 20, 1795. "The Senate, after a few weeks consultation, ratified the Treaty as you have seen. The injunction of secrecy was then dissolved by a full House, and quickly after restored sub modo, in a thin one. Mr. Mason, disregarding the latter vote, sent the Treaty to the press, from whence it flew with an electric velocity to every part of the Union." *Writings of James Madison*, VI. 258. This statement overlooks the fact that on the twenty-sixth practically the same motion that was reconsidered on the twenty-fifth was again passed, and that it did not remove the injunction against allowing the printing of the treaty. Some corroboration for Madison's statement about the reconsidering of the original motion in a thin house may be found in the circumstances that reconsideration was had upon motion of King, supported by Cabot and that it was ordered that all absent Senators be notified of the reconsideration.

of the members that this was a question which
should be left to the decision of the President.[1]
The pressure from without, however, was too heavy
to be withstood even by the compact body of thirty
men. As Oliver Wolcott put it, the permission
given was found to be equivalent to publication.
The contents of the mysterious document gradually
spread abroad,[2] and after the appearance of an incomplete sketch in the *Aurora*, Senator Stevens T.
Mason of Virginia sent his copy of the treaty to
the editor of that newspaper.[3] Thus the Senate
found itself unable to enforce secrecy upon all of

[1] On June 30 Hamilton wrote to Oliver Wolcott, "I find the
non-publication of the treaty is working as I expected — that is,
giving much scope to misrepresentation and misapprehension.
The Senate, I am informed by several members, did not take any step
towards publication, because they thought it the affair of the President to do as he thought fit." Hamilton to Wolcott, June 3. *Works
of Alexander Hamilton*, X. 107.

[2] On June 12, Pierce Butler, one of the Senators from South
Carolina, wrote Madison that he would send him by each post a
sheet of the treaty until he had received the whole. *Writings of
James Madison*, VI, 234n. Madison *MSS.* quoted as source.
Wolcott, with humor that perhaps is unintentional seems to have
expressed pretty accurately the attitude of the Senate on the question of publication in a letter written June 25 to his wife in which he
said, "The Senate have substantially ratified the treaty, though as
one point is suspended, it may be considered open. I understand
they have determined not to countenance a publication, though they
have reserved the right of conversing generally about it. Perhaps
this will be found equivalent to a publication." Oliver Wolcott to
Mrs. Wolcott, June 25, 1795. Gibbs, *Administrations of Washington,
and Adams*, I. 199. Four days later Wolcott wrote to his father
enclosing a paper which contained the substance of the treaty with
the comment, "the curiosity of the public and the impossibility
of keeping absolute secrecy has induced a compromise, that the
treaty may be communicated informally to the public." Oliver
Wolcott to Oliver Wolcott Sr., June 29, 1795, *Ibid.*, I. 202.

[3] McMaster, *History of the People*, II. 216.

its members. Nor did it ever take any steps to
call to account the one who had ignored the injunction laid upon all. The special session was over
before the act was done. The publication seems to
have had little political effect, and when Congress
convened the following December no steps were
taken to censure the erring Senator from Virginia.[1]

The most significant of the points at which the
Jay treaty bears upon the development of the treaty-
making powers of the Senate may be summarized
in two groups, the first concerning the relation of
the Senate to the negotiation of the treaty, and the
second regarding their action in consenting to its
ratification.

In the first group may be considered Washington's
policy in communicating to Congress information
concerning British-American affairs. Almost from
the beginning of the government he kept both
houses of Congress well informed upon the relations between this country and England. In a
number of instances, however, the Senate was given
more detailed and complete reports of the situation

[1] On May 4, 1796, an article which was explanatory to the third
article of the treaty of 1794 was signed at Washington by Phineas
Bond, His Majesty's Chargé d'Affaires, and Timothy Pickering,
Secretary of State. The article provided that nothing in any
treaty subsequently entered into by either nation with a third
nation or any Indian tribe should derogate in any manner from
the rights of passage across the American Canadian border and
the right to carry on trade across the border as guaranteed by
Article 3. Great Britain had deemed these rights to be threatened by Article 8 of the Treaty of Greenville. The additional
article was sent to the Senate on the day following its signature and
advice and consent to its ratification was given four days later.
Sen. Exec. Jour., I. 207.

than were vouchsafed the House, which course has become customary.

Probably the outstanding point in connection with the negotiation of the treaty, however, is the extent to which a small group of Federalist Senators, who were also among Washington's most trusted advisers, dominated the entire proceeding. These men suggested the mission; they secured its acceptance by the President, and practically directed the selection of the envoy; they secured his confirmation by the Senate; they sent him out fully cognizant with their views as to what sort of a treaty should be striven for and under very flexible instructions from the Department of State.

It is also important to remember that this group prevailed upon the Senate to approve the general purpose of tHe mission by confirming the nomination of the envoy without demanding to be informed of and to pass judgment upon the particular instructions under which the negotiation was to be carried on.

Many points in the procedure of the Senate after the treaty had been laid before them are worthy of note. Again the influence of the same leaders, possessing the confidence both of the Senate and of the President, was sufficient to control the situation and largely determined the action of the Senate throughout the session. It was under their influence that the Senate consented to the ratification of the treaty, only upon condition that the twelfth article be amended. It was then decided that such conditional ratification was to be considered as the final act of the Senate; and that it was not necessary to resubmit the treaty to the Senate after their amendments had been accepted by the executive and the other signatory power. The conditional ratification of the treaty was acceded to by England without protest.

Of much importance was the refusal of the Senate to adopt a resolution that the President be requested to renegotiate the treaty. This refusal, taken in conjunction with its earlier action in voting down a resolution demanding Jay's instructions, must have confirmed Washington in his conclusion that it was both constitutional and expedient to consult the Senate through influential members during the earlier processes of treaty-making, and to seek its formal approval of treaties only at the time of ratification, rather than prior to and during the period of negotiation. His experience with the Senate in connection with Indian treaties had led him to adopt this policy, and, by not challenging it in this important instance, the Senate may be considered to have sanctioned the practice.

Finally, by failing to maintain secrecy with reference to the treaty, the Senate seemed to justify the opinion of Washington that it was not a safe repository for diplomatic secrets. This question has been a delicate point between the Senate and the President at various times since Washington's day.

The participation of the Senate in making the Jay treaty illustrates the process by which governmental powers and institutions are developed. The permanent procedure of the Senate for the consideration of treaties, its relations with the President in this matter, and the exemption of the United States from the rule that a nation is ordinarily bound to ratify treaties signed by its plenipotentiaries were largely determined by the course followed at this time. Yet not constitutional theory but rather the exigencies of national and international politics governed the action of all parties to the transaction. Thus constitutional precedents which in time came to have great weight were by-products of the political process. Recognition of this fact does not decrease the importance of the procedure which here was in the making. On the contrary, it gives to procedure a living quality which it never can possess of itself.

CHAPTER V

THE CREEK TREATY OF 1796

THE last important treaty which Washington sent to the Senate was that signed with the Creek nation at Coleraine June 29, 1796. Six years previously a treaty concluded at New York had guaranteed to the Creeks all lands within the United States to the westward and southward of the boundary therein set up between them and the State of Georgia.[1] But this guarantee was believed by most Georgians to be beyond the powers of the central government and an infringement upon the rights of the state as sovereign over the territory in question.[2] On account of this feeling in Georgia, and for other reasons, the treaty had failed to settle the Creek question. So, after four years of disorder along the frontier, the state legislature in December, 1794, instructed the Georgia representatives in Congress to apply to the federal government to make a treaty securing from the Creeks the cession of those lands lying beyond the existing boundary line and between the Oconee and the Ocmulgee rivers.[3] Before this request was preferred, the

[1] *Am. State Papers, Indian Affairs*, I. 82, Art. 5, Treaty, August 7, 1790.

[2] *Ibid.*, I. 560, 561.

[3] Phillips, *Georgia and State Rights*, Ch. II.

95

Georgia legislature had passed an act authorizing the Yazoo land sale and declaring that the state possessed the right of preëmption of the Creek lands.[1] This action on the part of Georgia had been called to the attention of Congress by the President,[2] and in pursuance of a resolution of both houses an inquiry into the subject had been instituted.[3] Therefore, when the request of Georgia was laid before Washington near the end of the session in the spring of 1795, it asked for action which involved questions affecting the general policy to be pursued towards the Creeks, the ultimate rights of Georgia over the Indian lands, and, indirectly, the attitude of the Federal Government toward the Yazoo sale. The delicacy of the situation and the complexity and importance of the issues involved led the President to hold the matter over until the end of the special session of the Senate which was called to consider the Jay treaty.

On the day following the final action of the Senate on this treaty Washington laid the Georgia-Creek matter before it. He stated that he had decided to accede to the request of the state, but with the explicit declaration that neither his assent nor any treaty which might be made should be considered as affecting any question arising under the act of sale of the Georgia assembly of January 7, 1795, and that any cession of Indian claims should be made in the language of the treaty of New York.

[1] Phillips, *Georgia and State Rights*, p. 30. The act was signed January 7, 1795.

[2] Richardson, *Messages*, I. 175.

[3] President's Message, June 25, 1795, *Am. State Papers, Indian Affairs*, I. 560.

It also was to be required that Georgia pay one-half of the expense incident to the negotiations. Washington further stated that this seemed to be a favorable opportunity to inquire into all of the causes of dissatisfaction among the Creeks, and that

The commissioners for holding the proposed treaty will, therefore, be instructed to inquire into the causes of the hostilities to which I have referred, and to enter into such reasonable stipulations as will remove them, and give permanent peace to those parts of the United States.

The nomination of three commissioners followed,[1] and the last act of the special session was their unanimous confirmation.[2]

Six months later the President laid before the Senate the signed treaty.[3] Although successful in concluding a treaty of peace which proved to be lasting in its effect, the commissioners not only had failed to secure the desired cession of land for Georgia, but they had included in the treaty provisions which aroused the determined opposition of that state.

Articles three and four provided that the President should have the power to establish trading or military posts in the territory of the Creeks for the purpose of preventing the violation of any of the provisions or regulations subsisting between the parties, and that the Indians should annex to each such post a tract of land five miles square and cede the same to the United States. It was further provided that when such lands were no longer necessary for the purpose for which they were ceded they

---

[1] *Sen. Exec. Jour.*, I. 189–190.   [2] *Ibid.*, p. 192.

[3] *Ibid.*, p. 219; *Am. State Papers, Indian Affairs*, 1. 586–616, for message, treaty, and documents submitted.

should revert to the Indians. At the conclusion of the negotiations at Coleraine the three commissioners whom the State of Georgia had sent to attend them prepared a protest against the treaty and against the manner in which it had been negotiated. The fifth of the seven points made was an objection to this cession of land to the United States without the consent of Georgia. The act was declared to be in contravention of Section 8 of Article I of the Constitution.[1]

The protest of the Georgia commissioners was submitted to the Senate along with a voluminous record of the negotiations. In all, the documents bulked to some forty thousand words. After five days spent in going through this mass of material the matter was referred to a committee composed of Read of South Carolina, Sedgwick of Massachusetts, and Ross of Pennsylvania.[2] This committee recommended that the treaty be ratified with the proviso that nothing in the third and fourth articles should be construed to affect any claim of the State of Georgia to the right of preëmption in the land therein set apart for military or trading posts; "or after the Indian rights to the lands adjoining thereto shall have been legally extinguished by the State of Georgia, to give to the United States without the consent of the said State, a right to the soil, or the exclusive legislation over the same."[3]

This report was considered in five separate executive sessions.[4] Then an amendment was intro-

---

[1] *Am. State Papers, Indian Affairs*, I. 613–614.
[2] *Sen. Exec. Jour.*, I. 220–221.   [3] *Ibid.*, p. 222.
[4] *Ibid.*, pp. 222, 225, 226.

duced striking out of the treaty so much of the third and fourth articles as provided for the cession of land to the United States.[1] The Senate, however, was not ready to admit the contentions of Georgia to this extent, and the proposed amendment was voted down.[2] The protection of whatever rights Georgia had to the land in question was made more explicit, however, by amending the last part of the resolution reported by the committee so that it declared that nothing in the two articles should be construed

to give to the United States, without the consent of the said State, any right to the soil, or the exclusive legislation over the same, or any other right than that of establishing, maintaining and exclusively governing, military and trading posts within the Indian territory mentioned in the said articles as long as the frontier of Georgia may require these establishments.

The advice and consent of the Senate to the ratification of the treaty was then given with this proviso and condition.[3]

Thus the Senate exercised its power in behalf of a state which felt that its rights were threatened by a treaty concluded by the executive.[4] Too much significance, however, should not be attached to its action in partially upholding the contentions of Georgia. There is no evidence that the executive opposed the proviso that finally was included in the Senate resolution. In fact, the original resolution

---

[1] *Sen. Exec. Jour.*, I. 227.   [2] *Ibid.*, pp. 229–230.   [3] *Ibid.*, pp. 229.

[4] It will be remembered that the treaty of Fort Harmar with the Six Nations was not acted upon by the Senate because that body feared that it infringed the rights of New York and Massachusetts to Indian lands. See pp. 15–16 above.

to protect the rights of Georgia was proposed by a committee two of whose three members were administration men. The amendment to nullify the Indian cessions completely, which was supported by the Georgia senators and seven of their Republican friends, was defeated 22 to 9. And that the conditional ratification finally advised was unsatisfactory to the state is shown by the fact that it was opposed by both of her senators and by six other Southerners. Thus, although the protesting state received some concessions from the Senate, there is nothing to indicate that it was given anything more than the executive was willing to grant; and certainly the condition with which ratification was consented to did not materially alter the character of the cessions which were protested against.[1] Upon this occasion, nevertheless, the Senate was the forum in which a state was able to appear and protest against an alleged invasion of its rights by the federal government; and if it did not receive all of the relief it asked for, it at least secured a very thorough discussion of its case [2] and a more explicit statement of the rights which the original treaty had intended to recognize.

[1] The instructions under which the Treaty of Coleraine was negotiated are not available. It is not unlikely, however, that in providing for the cessions in the form that they did the commissioners were acting upon their own responsibility and that the executive was glad to have this form modified by the Senate.

[2] The Treaty of Coleraine was considered by the Senate in thirteen separate executive sessions, and apparently some of the discussions were lengthy. As the treaty was comparatively brief, and as no other point seems to have aroused particular opposition, it is probable that most of this time was consumed in debating the objections of Georgia to the third and fourth paragraphs.

THE ADVICE OF THE SENATE UPON THE
EXECUTION OF TWO TREATIES

In addition to participating in the negotiation
and the ratification of treaties, the Senate was
called upon by Washington to assist in the interpretation of one treaty and to advise upon the manner
in which another should be carried out. The first
instance occurred in 1791. In January of that year
the President laid before the Senate a representation
of the Chargé d'Affaires of France that acts of
Congress of 1789 and 1790 imposing an extraordinary
tonnage on foreign vessels, without excepting those
of France, were in contravention of Article V of
the Treaty of Amity and Commerce of 1778. The
report of the Secretary of State, which accompanied
the representation, thoroughly discussed the case
from the viewpoint of American interests, and concluded by the presentation of three alternative
courses of action: (1) To insist upon the American
construction of the article in question, and to explain in friendly terms the difficulties involved in
the exemption claimed by France. (2) To agree
with the French interpretation and to modify the
law accordingly. (3) To waive the matter of right
and make the amendment as an act of friendship.[1]

The President submitted the report and the
documents to the consideration of the Senate that
he might "be enabled to give to it such answer as
may best comport with the justice and the interests
of the United States.[2]" The message was referred
to Morris, King, Izard, Strong, and Ellsworth.[3]

[1] *Sen. Exec. Jour.*, I. 65 *et seq.*   [2] *Ibid.*, pp. 65–72.   [3] *Ibid.*

After considering the report of this committee during several executive sessions, the Senate expressed the opinion that the American interpretation of the treaty was correct, and resolved, "That the Senate do advise that an answer be given to the Court of France, defending, in the most friendly manner, this construction in opposition to that urged by the said Court." [1] This course was adopted by the executive.

In January, 1797, the President sent to both Houses of Congress, in confidence, reports from the Departments of State and the Treasury which disclosed the fact that the appropriation made for carrying into effect the treaty with Algiers was inadequate for this purpose. $376,505.66 was the sum declared to be necessary for complying with the terms of the treaty.[2] This sum included the cost of a frigate not provided for in the agreement, but subsequently promised to the Dey. In the Senate this message and the accompanying documents were referred to a committee composed of Marshall, Goodhue, and Tichenor.[3] The committee submitted a report, which was adopted, recommending that the money should be appropriated,[4] and approving the agreement to add a frigate to the naval equipment promised the Dey. Although the message of the President was received, discussed, and acted upon in executive session, the House bill appropriating the money asked for was referred to another committee, and passed through the regular legisla-

[1] *Sen. Exec. Jour.*, I. 77.
[2] *Am. State Papers, For. Rels.*, X. 553–558.
[3] *Sen. Exec. Jour.*, I. 220.   [4] *Ibid.*, p. 225.

tive procedure.[1] The incident illustrates how, even
at this period, the Senate was developing a special,
or separate, procedure for matters relating to foreign
affairs.

SUMMARY

A review of Washington's administrations reveals
several distinct developments in the interpretation
and application of the treaty-making clause.   There
can be no doubt that from the very beginning the
Senate exercised to the full the powers in treaty-
making and in foreign affairs granted to it by the
Constitution.   The Senate of Washington's administrations was a compact body of experienced
and able statesmen.   Foreign affairs and relations
with the Indian tribes were among the most important of the subjects with which the new government had to deal.   Through the constant exercise
of its treaty-making powers the Senate exerted a
powerful influence in both fields of activity.   It advised the opening of negotiations, passed upon the
instructions under which they were to be carried on,
and in some instances amended or rejected treaties
already made.   Washington made treaties "by and
with the advice and consent" of the Senate in a
sense and to an extent that no later President ever
has.

One very important decision reached by the logic
of events during these eight years, however, was
that the Senate could not really be a "council of
advice" to the President in treaty-making.   Yet

[1] *Annals of Congress*, 1796–1797, pp. 1556, 1559, 1567, 1570–
1571.

evidently both Washington and the Senate originally
expected that it would be such a council. The
personal element in their relations was emphasized
by the presence of the Secretary of State or the
Secretary of War, or, in the one instance, of the
President himself at their deliberations. Washington expressed it as his opinion that personal conferences were indispensably necessary in treaty
matters, and provision was made for such conferences. The chief result of the first conference was
that it was the last. Messages on treaty matters
came to be transmitted to the Senate by the President's private secretary, and communications between the Senate and the heads of departments
took on a formal and impersonal tone. Such, in
fact, came to be the general character of the relations between the President and his cabinet, and the
Senate in the performance of their joint function.

As the Senate ceased to be consulted as a real
"council of advice" its activities in that part of
treaty-making known as the negotiation became less
important. At first in making treaties both with
the Indian tribes and with foreign nations the
President usually secured the advice and consent
of the Senate to the details of the proposed treaty
before opening the negotiation. In the end it became his custom merely to inform the Senate of
the proposed negotiation upon securing its consent
to the nomination of the agent, and to submit the
latter's instructions only with the completed treaty.
The vast difference between the detailed manner in
which the advice of the Senate was taken prior to
the negotiation of the Creek treaty of 1790 and the

brief statement in which the President made known to them his intention to settle the differences between those Indians and the United States in 1796, is typical of the change in procedure. The same development is illustrated by comparing the relations of the Senate and the President in making the Spanish treaty with the manner in which the Jay treaty was made. In the former instance the President laid before the Senate a definite, and, as to some subjects, a detailed statement of the treaty he intended to secure. The Senate agreed to consent to the ratification of any treaty signed in accordance with these propositions. In the latter case John Jay was nominated as envoy to England to "adjust our complaints" against that country. The Senate was not informed of the particular measures he was to take to attain this end, nor was it bound to accept the resulting treaty. The effect of the change in procedure was to leave the President free to negotiate the sort of treaty which the necessities of the situation demanded and allowed, while the Senate retained a like freedom to accept, to amend, or to reject the result of his efforts.

The principle of independence, however, if carried too far, obviously would have produced an unsatisfactory, if not an unworkable, system. But along with this method of procedure there developed another factor which tended to modify its separative effects. This factor was the committee. During the period under consideration the development of the committee system with reference to foreign affairs was spontaneous and not the result of conscious effort on the part of the Senate. In the case of the Jay treaty, in which a small group of Senators secured a reasonable degree of unity between the Senate and the President, the essential principle of the committee system was applied naturally, but informally, perhaps unknowingly. The need existed; it was met in the most natural, direct, and simple manner. As later developed, the committee system became the recognized substitute for the abandoned practice of personal consultation between the Senate and the President in treaty-making. During these first eight years, however, committees were utilized in treaty matters primarily to expedite and make more effective the work of the Senate in this field, rather than as a means of contact between the two parties to the treaty-making power.

CHAPTER VI

Treaties of the Administration of John Adams

Two of the treaties which came before the Senate during the John Adams administration may be considered very briefly. The first was the Treaty of Peace and Friendship with Tripoli, signed the fourth of November, 1796.[1] The second was an article explanatory of the Jay treaty, releasing the commissioners under the fifth article from particularizing the latitude and longitude of the River St. Croix.[2] The Tripolitan treaty was submitted at the end of May, 1797, while the explanatory article was received just a year later. The procedure upon the two treaties was identical except at one point. Each was read and on a subsequent day referred to a committee of three; in each case the committee reported favorably and the resolution of advice and consent was agreed to without a dissenting vote. The single difference is that the treaty with Tripoli was ordered to be printed immediately after being read, while no such order was entered with reference to the explanatory article. By this time it had become the usual custom to order treaties to be printed

[1] *Am. State Papers, For. Rels.,* II. 18; *Sen. Exec. Jour.,* I. 241, 244.

[2] *Ibid.,* pp. 278–9.

in confidence for the use of the Senate, although as yet the practice was not invariable.

THE TREATY OF 1797 WITH TUNIS

On February 21, 1798, the President laid before the Senate a treaty of "Peace, Friendship, Commerce and Navigation" with the Bey of Tunis.[1] This treaty had been negotiated for the United States by Joseph S. Famin, a French merchant, acting under instructions from Joel Barlow, Consul General at Algiers. It was intended to secure American shipping in the Mediterranean from molestation by Tunisian corsairs and to regulate the commerce between the two countries.[2] It was in connection with one of the provisions upon the latter subject that the Senate interposed its authority to protect the United States from the results of a serious diplomatic error.

Immediately after having been read, the message and the treaty were referred to a committee composed of Bingham of Pennsylvania, Read of South Carolina, and Sedgwick of Massachusetts.[3] They reported a resolution advising and consenting to the ratification of the treaty on condition that the fourteenth article be suspended and recommending that the President enter into further negotiations with the Bey "on the subject of the said article, so

[1] *Sen. Exec. Jour.*, I. 262. For discussion of the treaty see Lyman, *Diplomacy of the United States*, II. 396–402; Allen, *Our Navy and the Barbary Corsairs*, pp. 59–66.

[2] For original treaty and documents submitted therewith see *Am. State Papers, For. Rels.*, II. 123–125.

[3] *Sen. Exec. Jour.*, I. 262.

as to accommodate the provisions thereof, to the existing treaties of the United States with other nations." This resolution was adopted.[1]

The article which was thus suspended by the Senate was intended to regulate the customs duties between the two countries. It read as follows:

The Citizens of the United States of America, who shall transport into Tunis the merchandise of their country, in the vessels of their nation, shall pay three per cent. duty. Such as may be laden by such citizens under a foreign flag coming from the United States, or elsewhere, shall pay ten per cent. duty. Such as may be laden by foreigners on American vessels coming from any place whatever, shall also pay ten per cent. duty. If any Tunisian merchant wishes to carry merchandise of his country, under any flag whatever, into the United States of America, and on his own account, he shall pay three per cent. duty.[2]

The Senate found two objections to this article. First, the provisions governing the duties to be paid by citizens of the two states, respectively, upon goods carried into the other violated the principle that treaties should be reciprocal in their terms. These provisions, however, probably were of little practical importance, inasmuch as the amount of goods brought into the United States by the merchants of Tunis was, and might be expected to remain, small.

The second objection was a more serious one. It was based upon a direct conflict between the last provision of the article in question and the most favored nation clause in our treaties with other

[1] *Sen. Exec. Jour.*, I. 263–264.
[2] *Am. State Papers, For. Rels.*, II. 124.

nations. Its probable effect upon the United States, had it been enforced, is clearly set forth in the following paragraph from the instructions under which the negotiations for its alteration were carried on:

The revenues of the United States arise chiefly from duties on goods imported. The duties generally exceed ten per cent. They are imposed on our own merchants, and increased on the merchants of foreign nations. Our treaties with these nations state that no higher duties shall be paid by their subjects than by those of the most favored nation. Consequently, if this article in the Treaty with Tunis should be ratified by the American Government, the duties on all the goods imported into the United States by the subjects of these foreign nations must be reduced to three per cent. This would necessarily involve the reduction of the duties on goods imported in our own vessels, or our whole navigation would sink beneath the unequal burthen.[1]

In December, 1799, the President informed the Senate that in accordance with their recommendation he had entered into a further negotiation with the Bey on the subject of the fourteenth article of the treaty, and laid the result of the negotiation before them.[2] In addition to the modification of the article which was rejected by the Senate, the new negotiation had resulted in alterations to the eleventh and twelfth articles.[3]

[1] Instructions to Richard O'Brien, William Eaton, and James Leander Cathcart, *Am. State Papers, For. Rels.*, II. 281.

[2] *Sen. Exec. Jour.*, I. 328.

[3] The eleventh article had provided that upon entering the port of one of the parties a war vessel of the other should be saluted by the fort and should return the salute, gun for gun; also that she should give to the authorities of the port a barrel of powder for each gun fired. It was well known that no war vessel of Tunis would be

The Senate referred the matter to the committee which had recently been appointed to consider the treaty with Prussia. The reference to this committee is explained by the fact that Bingham, its chairman, and one other member had served on the committee upon the original treaty with Tunis, of which Bingham had been chairman. A few days later the Senate gave its advice and consent to the ratification of the three articles in question.[1]

There seem to be no means of ascertaining whether the action of the Senate in suspending the fourteenth article of this treaty was spontaneous or whether the recommendation of the original committee sprang from a suggestion from the State Department or the President. It is obvious, however, that the Senate gave to the government of the United States an opportunity to propose the necessary alteration upon grounds that Tunis could not reasonably take exception to. The change in itself was of the greatest importance. Had the treaty been ratified as signed, the United States undoubtedly would

likely to enter an American port, while the almost constant presence of American cruisers in the Mediterranean could thus be made to furnish the Bey with a fairly steady supply of powder — particularly as the number of guns to be fired was unlimited. In the revised article it is provided that the salute should not be fired by the forts except at the request of the American consul; that the number of guns should be fired which he might request; and, "if the said Consul does not want a salute, there shall be no question about it." Article XI, Treaty of Amity, Commerce and Navigation, Tunis, 1797. *Treaties, Conventions, International Acts, Protocols and Agreements Between the United States of America and Other Powers*, 1776–1909 (Sen. Doc., No. 357, 61st Cong. 2d Session), p. 1796.

[1] *Sen. Exec. Jour.*, I. 328–330.

have been compelled to secure its abrogation or alteration as soon as the other nations with which we had treaty relations discovered the terms of the fourteenth article.

THE TREATY OF 1799 WITH PRUSSIA

Senate action on the treaty of 1799 with Prussia adds but little to a study of the development of the treaty-making power. This treaty was practically a renewal, with modifications, of the Prussian treaty of 1785, and in itself seems to have been acceptable to the Senate. The nomination of the negotiator, John Quincy Adams, as minister plenipotentiary to Prussia, was opposed by more than a third of the Senate but this opposition seems to have been directed primarily at the establishment of a permanent minister at the Court of Prussia. Adams was confirmed in May, 1797,[1] and the treaty which he negotiated was submitted to the Senate in December, 1799. It was ordered to be printed, and three days later was referred to a committee composed of Bingham of Pennsylvania, Dexter of Massachusetts, Watson of New York, Read of South Carolina, and Goodhue of Massachusetts. Late in January this committee reported a resolution of advice and consent to ratification. Before adopting the report, the Senate, after extended debate, passed a resolution asking for the instructions given to Adams and for the correspondence respecting the negotiation. The papers were submitted on February 17, and on the day following, the

[1] *Sen. Exec. Jour.*, I. 240–242.

Senate voted to advise and consent to ratification, 26 to 6.[1]

Although in the case of the Prussian treaty the disapprobation of a large minority of Senators to the nomination of a minister did not extend to the treaty which that minister was to negotiate, it is evident that the influence which this means of expressing disapproval of a treaty might exert upon the executive was well understood at the time. That it was realized is clearly shown by the action of certain Senators with reference to the nomination of John Quincy Adams in 1798 as commissioner to secure a treaty of amity and commerce with Sweden. The nomination was sent in on March 12. Two days later it was confirmed, 20 to 8.[2] On the following day Jefferson wrote to his friend Madison as follows:

The President has nominated John Quincy Adams Commissioner Plenipotentiary to renew the treaty with Sweden. Tazewell made a great stand against it, on the general ground that we should let our treaties drop, and remain without any. He could only get eight votes against twenty. A trial will be made today in another form, which he thinks will give ten or twelve against sixteen or seventeen, declaring the renewal inexpedient. In this case, notwithstanding the nomination has been confirmed, it is supposed the President would perhaps not act under it, on the probability that more than a third would be against ratification. I believe, however, that he would act, and that a third could not be got to oppose the ratification.[3]

[1] Sen. Exec. Jour., I. 326, 327, 337-340; Am. State Papers, For. Rels., II. 244-268; Lyman, Diplomacy of the United States, I. 150-153, discusses the policy involved in renewing the treaty.

[2] Sen. Exec. Jour., I. 266.

[3] Jefferson to Madison, March 15, 1798. Writings of Thomas Jefferson, X. 8.

The journals of the Senate disclose no such attempt on the part of Tazewell; possibly he had become convinced of the futility of his opposition. But in any event the incident shows clearly that at the time it was recognized that a strong minority could, if it desired, adopt this means of discouraging the undertaking of any negotiation of which it disapproved.

SENATE AMENDMENTS TO THE TREATY OF 1800 WITH FRANCE

The action of the Senate in connection with the treaty with France of September 30, 1800, is of importance for two reasons. First, the manner in which the Senate amended the convention is a striking example of the extent to which that body can influence the treaty stipulations and affect the foreign policy of the United States. Second, it was during the consideration of this convention that the Senate adopted its first set of rules formally setting forth the procedure to be followed when a treaty should be laid before it for ratification.

The political and commercial relations between the United States and France had been defined by the treaties of amity and commerce, and of alliance of 1778, and by the consular convention which had been ratified in 1789. Changing conditions, however, made the stipulations of these treaties difficult to fulfill, particularly for the United States. Between 1790 and 1798, the two republics passed from disagreement and mutual recrimination to *de facto*, if not *de jure* war. Congress, in July, 1798, by law declared the treaties of 1778 and the consular convention to be abrogated.[1] In February, 1799, in response to advances made by the French government, the President nominated Oliver Ellsworth, Chief Justice of the United States, Patrick Henry, ex-Governor of Virginia and William Vans Murray, Minister Resident at the Hague, "to be Envoys Extraordinary and Ministers Plenipotentiary to the French Republic, with full powers to discuss and settle, by treaty, all controversies between the United States and France." [2] In December, 1799, William R. Davie, Governor of North Carolina, was substituted for Henry.[3]

Secretary Pickering's instructions to these envoys directed that at the opening of the negotiation they should,[4]

inform the French ministers, that the United States expect from France, as an indispensable condition of the treaty, a stipulation to make to the citizens of the United States full compensation for all losses and damages which they shall have sustained by reason of irregular or illegal captures or condemnations of their vessels and other property, under color or authority of commissions from the French republic or its agents. And all captures and

[1] *United States Statutes at Large*, I, 578 (Acts of 2d Sess. of 5th Cong., Ch. XLVII).

[2] *Sen. Exec. Jour.*, I. 317.   [3] *Ibid.*, pp. 326–327.

[4] These instructions, the convention, and the other papers submitted to the Senate are printed in *Am. State Papers, For. Rels.*, I. 295–345. In Moore, *International Law Digest*, V. Sec. 821, is to be found one of the best brief accounts of our treaty relations with France, and perhaps the clearest statement of the action of the Senate with reference to this treaty. See also Davis, *Notes to Foreign Treaties*, pp. 1306–1307; Lyman, *Diplomacy of the United States*, I. viii; McMaster, *History of the People*, II. 527–529; Foster, *Century of American Diplomacy*, Ch. V.

condemnations are deemed irregular or illegal, when contrary to the law of nations generally received and acknowledged in Europe, and to the stipulations of the treaty of amity and commerce, of the 6th of February, 1778, fairly and ingenuously interpreted, while that treaty remained in force.[1]

And at the conclusion of the instructions it is stated that the seven points are "to be considered as ultimated." Of these the first is,

That an article be inserted for establishing a board, with suitable powers, to hear and determine the claims of our citizens, for the causes herein before expressed, and binding France to pay or secure payment of the sums which shall be awarded.

The second point is,

That the treaties and consular convention, declared to be no longer obligatory by act of Congress, be not in whole or in part revived by the new treaty; but that all the engagements to which the United States are to become parties, be specified in the new treaty.

The seventh stipulation is that with the exception of certain specified provisions, the duration of the proposed treaty be limited to not more than twelve years.[2]

When, during the following summer the American envoys met the citizen ministers appointed by the First Consul to treat with them, it was found that France was determined to agree to neither of the two chief objects which they had been instructed to secure. Joseph Bonaparte and his colleagues insisted that the ancient treaties were still in force,

---

[1] *Am. State Papers, For. Rels.*, II. 302.   [2] *Ibid.*, p. 306.

and denied that France was liable for any of the indemnities demanded for injuries to American shipping. An appeal to Napoleon, then in Italy, brought fresh instructions to his negotiators. In their own words, his proposition was "reduced to this simple alternative: Either the ancient treaties, carrying with them the privileges resulting from anteriority, together with stipulations for reciprocal indemnity; Or a new treaty, promising equality, unattended with indemnities." [1]

Napoleon, in effect, had given the Americans their choice of the two objects which they had been instructed to secure; they could not have both. Nor could he be moved from this position. A month later the American ministers became convinced of this fact. Not having authority either to give up the claims for indemnity or to admit the present validity of the treaties which their government had declared to be no longer binding upon the United States or its citizens, they determined to conclude a temporary arrangement upon both subjects. It was proposed that permanent settlement be "postponed until it can be resumed with fewer embarrassments." [2] The result of this decision was Article 2 of the treaty as signed September 30, 1800. This article was as follows:

The Ministers Plenipotentiary of the two parties not being able to agree, at present, respecting the treaty of alliance of 6th February, 1778, the treaty of amity and commerce of the same date and the convention of 14th of November, 1788, nor upon the indemnities mutually due or claimed; the parties will negotiate further upon

[1] *Am. State Papers, For. Rels.*, II. 332.   [1] *Ibid.*, p. 339.

these subjects at a convenient time, and until they may have agreed upon these points, the said treaties and convention shall have no operation, and the relations between the two countries shall be regulated as follows:[1] .

No limit was set to the duration of the convention. Moore states that with this exception, and that of compensation for condemnations and captures it substantially conformed to Pickering's ultimata.[2] The fact remained, however, that the two primary objects of the negotiation, the two questions which seemed of the utmost importance to almost every American of the day, were left unsettled. The executive had secured neither indemnity nor an abrogation of the treaties. What would the Senate do?

The Senate received the convention on December 16, 1800.[3] With it President Adams submitted the lengthy journal of the envoys, and a few days later, by request, the instructions under which the negotiators had acted. From the first the unpopularity of the treaty extended to the members of both parties. Three days after it was received Jefferson wrote to Madison that it would meet with opposition from both sides of the House; and he stigmatized it as the result of a "bungling negotiation."[4] A few days later Hamilton wrote from New York to Gouverneur Morris stating that several friends had informed him that there was "likely to be much hesitation in the Senate about ratifying the Con-

[1] *Am. State Papers, For. Rels.*, II., 295–296.

[2] Moore, *International Law Digest*, V. 611.

[3] *Sen. Exec. Jour.*, I. 359.

[4] Jefferson to Madison, December 19, 1800, *Writings of Thomas Jefferson*, X. 185.

vention." [1]   On the fifth of January, Pickering in a letter to Rufus King, stated, "It is reprobated by both parties, and if ratified it will be with exceptions." [2]

Almost exactly a month after it had been given into their hands the Senate referred the several votes which had been taken on the treaty to a committee composed of Morris, Nicholas, and Dayton with instructions to reduce them into the form of a ratification.[3] This proposed ratification showed that two-thirds of the Senators had voted for ratification with four provisos, as follows: 1. That the second article be expunged. 2. That the third article be expunged.[4] 3. That an article be inserted ex-

[1] Hamilton to G. Morris. *The Works of Alexander Hamilton* (Lodge ed.), X. 399. Hamilton thought that the convention should be ratified, "as the least of two evils."

[2] Pickering to King, January 5, 1801, *Life and Correspondence of Rufus King*, III. 366. On January 2, Senator McHenry, writing to his friend Rufus King, then our minister in London, said: "The convention lately entered into with France is before the Senate. Is it liked? No. As to its fate; some think it will be rejected; others that it will be accepted with modifications and exceptions; no one that it will be ratified as it is. McHenry to King, *Life and Correspondence of Rufus King*, III. 363.

Perhaps the strongest argument in favor of ratification was that the treaty at least would result in peace. This is graphically expressed by Pinckney, who wrote to Rufus King, December 27, 1800, "The treaty with the French Republic is before the Senate. . . . If it be ratified our little navy will be hauled up. Pickering to King, *Life and Correspondence of Rufus King*, III. 353.

[3] *Sen. Exec. Jour.*, I. 370.

[4] This article provided that public vessels which had been taken on either side, or which might be taken before the exchange of ratifications, should be restored. *Am. State Papers, For. Rels.*, II. 296. Although reciprocal in terms it militated against the United States and added to the unpopularity of the treaty. Senators and people were reluctant to return these "trophies of war."

pressing the understanding that nothing in the convention should be so construed to operate contrary to any former and existing treaties of either party. 4. That by an additional article it be stipulated that the duration of the convention should be eight years from the time of the exchange of ratifications. But when these questions were severally put to the Senate the fourth was the only one which received the constitutional majority; and the report, amended accordingly, failed, 16 to 14.[1] This was understood to mean the rejection of the treaty, and on the following Monday a resolution was introduced to make the action a formal one.[2]

A large majority of the senators, however, considered the treaty, with some amendments, to be better than the existing conditions and those which might follow its rejection.[3] Hamilton and other influential Federalists, including the President, urged its acceptance, probably on both party and national

---

[1] *Sen. Exec. Jour.*, I. 370, 373–4.   [2] *Ibid.*, p. 374.

[3] The following excerpts from the diary of Gouveneur Morris throw an interesting light on the action of the Senate at this point: "I go through the treaty in the House today," Morris says, January 15th "and agree to the amendments of the committee; some sharpness of debate. Report the form of a ratification; consideration postponed." On the 23d the Senate rejected the convention with France, "by the intemperate passion of its friends." By the 26th there was a general desire in the House "to recede from the vote as it stands on the convention. As I all along expected it will be reconsidered." *Diary and Letters of Gouverneur Morris* II. 399. A reconsideration, in fact, seems to have been generally expected. February 1, Pickering in relating to Rufus King the details of the rejection concluded, "It is suggested, however, as a thing to be expected from the Democrats, that a reconsideration may be proposed in order to ratify with conditions rather than lose the treaty." *Life and Correspondence of Rufus King*, III. 392.

grounds.[1] The result was that the advice and consent of the Senate was given to ratification with the provisos that the second article be expunged and that the convention should be limited in its operation to eight years from the time of the exchange of ratifications.

At this point a comparison should be made between the action of the Senate on the signed treaty, and that taken by the original negotiators upon the alternatives offered to them by Napoleon. A careful consideration of the second article convinced the Senate that it recognized the existence of the treaties which Congress had declared abrogated. The agreement was that at a future time the two governments should negotiate upon the abrogation of these treaties and the payment of indemnities; and that until then the "said treaties and conventions shall have no operation, and the relations between the two countries shall be regulated," in accordance with the remaining articles of the convention.[2] The American envoys, devoid

[1] Hamilton to G. Morris, *Works of Alexander Hamilton*, X. 398–400, December 24, 1800; also see Schouler, *History of the United States*, I. 477–479.

[2] On January 16, Morris wrote· to Hamilton, "As to the induction from the words of the second article, that the old treaties [subsisted] though their operation was suspended, I think it undeniable that, taken in consideration with other things, would have involved us in serious difficulty. . . . When, therefore, acknowledging their existence by suspending their effects generally, we particularly stipulate, and literally renew a part; might not the French demand for the part so renewed a *priority?* . . . · Those articles (the second and the third) being left out, the convention must be considered merely as a treaty of peace. The preëxistence of war is admitted, and from the moment of that admission there is an end to treaties and to claims of restitution and indemnity.

of authority to accept either one of the two alternatives offered by the French, had postponed the decision of both in a manner that seemed to have strengthened the French position with reference to the more important of the two questions — the status of the treaties.

The authority of the Senate, however, was plenary. By expunging the second article, in effect they accepted Napoleon's second proposition, namely, "the abrogation of ancient treaties; the formation of a new treaty, . . . and an entire silence on the subject of indemnities."

This amendment of the treaty put the next move up to the executive department. Three days before the end of the session Adams sent in a message in which he said:

> I have considered the advice and consent of the Senate, to the ratification of the convention with France, under certain conditions. Although it would have been more conformable to my own judgment and inclination, to have agreed to that instrument unconditionally, yet, as in this point, I found I had the misfortune to disagree from so high a constitutional authority as the Senate, I judged it more consistent with the honour and interest of the United States to ratify it under the conditions prescribed, than not at all.

He further stated that the matter of the exchange of ratifications was to be left to his successor.[1]

Nothing, therefore, can make the matter more clear than to be perfectly silent." Morris to Hamilton, January 16, 1801, *Diary and Letters of Gouverneur Morris*, II. 399–400. This letter was written on the day following the first vote of the Senate to expunge the second article.

[1] *Sen. Exec. Jour.*, I. 388. French ministers to the American envoys, August 11, 1800. *Am. State Papers, For. Rels.*, II. 332.

This exchange was affected by Jefferson. But in consenting to the adoption of the amendments suggested by the American Senate, Napoleon stipulated that by the expunction of the second article, "the two states renounce the respective pretensions which are the object of the said article." [1]   Thus the First Consul stated explicitly what had been implied by the action of the Senate. And that this was the understanding of the Senate and of the President is made evident by subsequent events. On December 11, 1801, Jefferson sent in the following message:

Early in the last month, I received the ratification, by the First Consul of France, of the convention between the United States and that nation. His ratification not being pure and simple, in the ordinary form, I have thought it my duty, in order to avoid all misconception, to ask a second advice and consent of the Senate, before I give it the last sanction, by proclaiming it to be a law of the land.[2]

[1] *Am. State Papers, For. Rels.*, II. 344.

[2] *Sen. Exec. Jour.*, I. 397; Jefferson's opinion that the stipulation made by Napoleon merely expressed what had been intended by the Senate when it rejected Article 3 is officially set forth in the following letter from Madison to Livingston: "As the form of ratification by the French Government contained a clause declaratory of the effect given to the meaning of the treaty by the supression of the second article, it was thought by the President most safe, as a precedent, to ask anew the sanction of the Senate to the instrument with that ingredient. No decision has yet been taken by that body; and from the novelty of the case, the number of absent members, and the delays incident to questions of form, it is possible that it may be some little time yet before the subject is brought to a conclusion. . . . I am authorized to say that the President does not regard the declaratory clause as more than a legitimate inference from the rejection by the Senate of the second article, and that he is deposed to go on with the measures due under

After careful consideration by a committee composed of Logan, Jackson, and Tracy, and in debate upon the floor in executive session, the Senate passed the following resolution:

Resolved, that the convention, as ratified by the first Consul of France, and declared to be considered by the Senate, two-thirds concurring thereto, to be fully ratified, be returned to the President of the United States, for the usual promulgation.[1]

This, it is to be noted, is not a second resolution of advice and consent, but a statement that in the opinion of the Senate the ratification of Napoleon, with its stipulation, did not call for new action by that body. Had the definite statement of Napoleon as to the effect of the expunction of the second article not been in accord with the former intentions of the Senate it is hardly likely that they would have failed to exercise their authority either to accept or to reject it, as an explanation of the treaty.

If the process of making this French Convention of 1800 be considered to extend from the nomination of the American envoys by the President to the final exchange of ratifications, the transaction illustrates the extent to which the Senate may participate in the actual negotiation of a treaty. The President initiated the negotiation and issued the instructions under which it was carried on. The agents of the executive, acting under these instructions, signed a convention which settled neither

the compact to the French Republic." Madison, Secretary of State, to Livingston, U. S. Minister to France, December 18, 1801, *Am. State Papers, For. Rels.*, VI. 155.

[1] *Sen. Exec. Jour.*, I. 397–399.

of the two cardinal points at issue between the two nations. The instrument as signed, however, was only the draft of a treaty. As such it was referred to the ratifying authority of each state for the action which alone could give it legal validity. A part of that authority in the United States, the Senate, declined to accept the proposed treaty as it stood.[1] After familiarizing themselves with the details of the negotiations, in effect the Senate went back to the point at which the French ministers had offered their alternative propositions, the ancient treaties with full indemnity, or a new treaty with no indemnity. Then, by striking out the second article, they did what the envoys could not do — they accepted the latter proposition. Also they limited the duration of the agreement to eight years.

The executive acceded to these propositions and laid them before the government of France. Napoleon, of course, was as free to accept them, to reject them, or to accept them conditionally as though they had been made during the course of the earlier negotiation. He saw fit to accede to them, with an explicit statement of what was implied by the excision of the second article. This acceptance on his part was recognized by the Senate as completing the ratification of the instrument.[2] If, on the other

---

[1] In this case there can be no question of the complete right of the United States to refuse to ratify what its agents had agreed to, for the reason that those agents had agreed to a convention which was not in accord with their instructions.

[2] That the Senate understood that in advising and consenting to a conditional ratification they were running the risk of losing the convention is made evident by the correspondence of leading Senators

hand, further conditions had been postulated by the First Consul these in turn might have come before the Senate for consideration.

RULES FOR PROCEDURE UPON TREATIES

It has been noted that from the moment of the submission of the French Convention of 1800, senators were aware that the struggle over its adoption would be a severe one. Perhaps this was the reason that during its consideration the first set of standing rules governing in detail procedure upon treaties was adopted. Along with the convention the President had submitted the journals of the American ministers. These were read through in three days, and Adams was then requested to lay before the Senate the instructions of the envoys.[1] In complying with this request he asked that the instructions be considered in strict confidence and that they be returned to him as soon as the Senate should have made all the use of them which they might judge necessary. The following resolution was then adopted:

Resolved, That all confidential communications made by the President of the United States to the Senate, shall be, by the members thereof, kept inviolably secret; and that all treaties which may hereafter be laid before the Senate,

on both sides. It therefore is to be assumed that the Senate preferred no treaty at all to that presented to them. See Hamilton to Morris, January 10, 1801, *Works of Alexander Hamilton*, X. 410, Pickering to King, January 5, 1801, *Life and Correspondence of Rufus King*, III. 366; G. Morris to Robert Livingston, February 20, 1801, *Diary and Letters of Gouverneur Morris*, II. 404.

[1] *Sen. Exec. Jour.*, I. 359–360.

shall also be kept secret, until the Senate shall by their resolution, take off the injunction of secrecy.[1]

Thus the Senate established a standing rule providing for the secret consideration of all treaties and all confidential communications from the President in relation to treaties or foreign affairs.

The next step in the formulation of procedure was taken early in January. After it had discussed the treaty for several weeks, and before balloting thereon, the Senate laid down the following general rule:

Resolved, (as a standing rule,) That whenever a treaty shall be laid before the Senate for ratification, it shall be read a first time, for information only; when no motion to reject, ratify, or modify, the whole, or any part, shall be received.

That its second reading shall be for consideration, and on a subsequent day, when it shall be taken up, as in a committee of the whole, and every one shall be free to move a question on any particular article, in this form — "Will the Senate advise and consent to the ratification of this article?" or to propose amendments thereto, either by inserting or by leaving out words; in which last case the question shall be, "Shall the words stand part of the article?" And in every of the said cases, the concurrence of two-thirds of the Senators present shall be requisite to decide affirmatively. And when through the whole, the proceedings shall be stated to the House, and questions be again severally put thereon for confirmation, or new ones proposed, requiring in like manner, a concurrence of two-thirds for whatever is retained or inserted.

That the votes so confirmed shall, by the House, or a committee thereof, be reduced into the form of a ratification, with or without modifications, as may have been decided, and shall be proposed on a subsequent day,

[1] *Sen. Exec. Jour.*, I. 361.

when everyone shall be free again to move amendments, either by inserting or leaving out words; in which last case, the question shall be, "Shall the words stand part of the resolution?" And in both cases the concurrence of two-thirds shall be requisite to carry the affirmative; as well as on the final question to advise and consent to the ratification, in the form agreed to.[1]

The provisions of this rule may be briefly summarized. Three readings on three different days are provided for. The first is for information only and at this time no motion to act upon the treaty or any part of it is in order. Nothing is said as to other motions, such as to refer to a committee, to request further information from the executive, and so on. The second reading is for consideration, debate, and balloting in the committee of the whole. All questions to ratify, amend, or reject any part of the treaty are to be decided by a two thirds vote. The same majority is made necessary for the acceptance by the House of each part of the report of the committee. It is then provided that the votes so confirmed shall be reduced into a form of ratification. This resolution shall in turn be submitted to debate, and shall be liable to amendment by two thirds vote. The final question to advise and consent to the ratification shall be on the form agreed to and a two thirds vote shall be necessary to carry the affirmative.

It has been noted that after the French convention had been rejected, the general sentiment of the Senate was in favor of a reconsideration. On February 3, accordingly, a rule was adopted which provided,

[1] *Sen. Exec. Jour.*, I. 365.

That when any question may have been decided by the Senate in which two-thirds of the members present are necessary to carry the affirmative, any member who voted on that side which prevailed in the question, may be at liberty to move for a reconsideration; and a motion for reconsideration shall be decided by a majority of votes.[1]

[1] *Sen. Exec. Jour.*, I. 376.

Section LII of *Jefferson's Manual* treats rather of the nature of the treaty-making power, and the relative powers of the President and the Senate therein than of the procedure of the Senate upon treaties laid before it. He refers to the usage in accordance with which the President was accustomed to communicate to the Senate the correspondence of the negotiators along with the treaty, and also states that the mode of voting on questions of ratification was by nominal call. *Senate Manual, Containing the Standing Rules and Orders of the United States Senate* (edition 1918), pp. 306–308.

Under the present rules, the procedure of the Senate on treaties is regulated by Rules XXXVI and XXXVII. Section three of the former enjoins secrecy upon senators in almost the same words as when adopted in 1801. The rule for proceedings on treaties has been altered in a number of details. The most important change is that which provides that a concurrence of two thirds of the Senators present shall be required to carry only the question of advice and consent to ratification, or to postpone indefinitely, other questions being carried by a simple majority. *Ibid.*, pp. 40–44.

CHAPTER VII

THE SENATE AND THE TREATIES OF THOMAS JEFFERSON

THE CONVENTION OF 1802 WITH SPAIN

THE proceedings of the Senate upon the claims convention of 1802 with Spain gave rise to several interesting developments. The treaty had been negotiated by Charles Pinckney, Minister of the United States in Madrid, under instructions to secure reparation from Spain for spoliations committed upon American commerce, principally during the naval war between the United States and France. Hundreds of American vessels had been captured by French privateers sailing from Spanish ports, and wrongfully condemned, either by Spanish tribunals, or by French consuls within Spanish jurisdiction.[1] Spain admitted responsibility for the acts of Spanish subjects, and the convention provided that claims arising out of spoliations by them should be adjudicated by a mixed commission

---

[1] *Am. State Papers, For. Rels.*, II. 476. Extract of a letter from the Secretary of State to Charles Pinckney. The correspondence and other documents connected with this convention will be found, *Ibid.*, pp. 440–458, 475–483, 596–608, 613–695. See also Davis, "Notes Upon Foreign Treaties of the United States," p. 1384; McMaster, *History of the People*, III. 34–36; Chadwick, *The Relations of the United States and Spain, Diplomacy*, p. 70, *et seq.*; Moore, *International Law Digest*, Vol. V., Sec. 821.

sitting in Madrid; but all rights arising under claims originating from the excesses of foreign cruisers, agents, consuls, or tribunals in the territories of either nation were to be reserved for future negotiation.

The convention was submitted to the Senate in January, 1803,[1] and was not finally passed upon until virtually a year thereafter. Soon after it was received, and again in March, the Senate took definitive action upon the treaty, but in each case reconsidered its decision.[2] Late in the following November, after the most pressing of the matters connected with the purchase of Louisiana had been disposed of, it resumed the consideration of the Spanish convention. Bradley, Jackson, and Baldwin were appointed a committee to inquire whether further proceedings by the Senate were necessary, and the convention was ordered to be printed.[3] This committee probably consulted with the President or with the Secretary of State, for on December 21 Jefferson sent in a message explaining the existing situation with reference to the treaty. The President stated that Pinckney had been instructed to press for an additional article comprehending French seizures and condemnations of American vessels in the ports of Spain. He also submitted correspondence which showed that this demand was being strongly resisted by the Spanish government, and suggested that it might be advisable to take what indemnities already had been conceded and negotiate on the other claims when

[1] *Sen. Exec. Jour.*, I. 435.   [2] *Ibid.*, 436–7, 441–8.
[3] *Ibid.*, p. 459.

the question of the boundaries of Louisiana came up for discussion.[1] This was also the opinion of the Senate, and on January 9 the convention was ratified as it stood, after the Federalist senators had vainly attempted to attach a condition that it should be understood to embrace all claims arising out of the action of Spanish subjects or American citizens, whether official or unofficial persons.[2]

In reviewing the action of the Senate as outlined above, attention should be directed to the reasons for its hesitation to act, to the results of the delay which this caused in the exchange of ratifications, and to two interesting phases of its procedure upon the convention. With reference to the first point, there can be no doubt as to the nature of the objections to the treaty. It was felt that no settlement should be made which did not bind Spain to make reparation for the loss of American ships carried into Spanish ports by French privateers or national vessels, and there condemned by French consuls.[3]

[1] *Sen. Exec. Jour.*, I. 461; *Am. State Papers, For. Rels*, II. 596–606.

[2] *Sen. Exec. Jour.*, I. 462.

[3] Immediately after the adjournment of Congress in March, 1803, Madison instructed Pinckney to press for the inclusion of these claims, saying, "More than a majority, but less than two-thirds, which constitution requires, would have acquiesced in the instrument in its present form; trusting to the success of further negotiations for supplying its defects, particularly the omission of the claims founded on French irregularities. But it is understood that it would have been a mere acquiescence, no doubt being entertained that Spain is bound to satisfy the omitted as well as the included claims. In explaining, therefore, the course taken by the Senate, which mingles respect for the Spanish government with a cautious regard for our own rights, you will avail yourself of the opportunity of pressing the reasonableness and sound policy of

The feeling on this point was so strong that the Senate seemed determined ·to consent to no treaty that did not provide for the settlement of both classes of claims.

The result of the year's delay in the ratification of this treaty by the United States was that no American claims were ever adjusted under it. During the interval occurred the cession of Louisiana, which increased the tension between this country and Spain; and after the passage of the Mobile Act, setting up a United States customs district in West Florida, Spain refused to ratify the treaty except under conditions to which the United States could not assent.[1] Ultimately, in 1818, Spain did ratify it unchanged, but it was annulled by Article X of the Treaty of 1819, before any action had been taken under it.[2]

In the matter of procedure two points of interest arise. The first is in connection with the opinion given by five eminent lawyers of Philadelphia and New York that Spain was under no obligation to make reparation for American vessels captured by French subjects and condemned in Spanish ports by French consuls. The question had been presented hypothetically by Spanish agents to Jared

remodelling the convention in such a manner as to do full justice." *Am. State Papers, For. Rels.*, II. 596.   In announcing the ratification of the convention to Robert R. Livingston, Minister to France, Madison wrote, "The objection to it was, that it did not provide in sufficient extent, for repairing the injuries done to our commerce, particularly in omitting the case of captures and condemnations by French cruisers and consuls, within Spanish responsibility. *Ibid.*, p. 614.

[1] Cevallos to Pinckney, July 2, 1804. *Ibid.*, p. 619.

[2] *Treaties and Conventions*, II. 1655.

Ingersoll, William Rawle, J. B. McKean, P. S. Duponceau, and Edward Livingston with a substitution of the letters A, B, and C for the names of Spain, France, and the United States. These gentlemen had agreed that Spain was not required by international law to pay the indemnities referred to. This opinion rested principally on the grounds, first, that Spain had been unable to prevent the spoliations, second that the claims in question had been released by the treaty of 1800 with France.[1] The signed opinion of these men was forwarded to the Spanish government, which used it to refute the arguments by which Pinckney sought to obtain an additional article covering these claims.[2]

The correspondence between Pinckney and Cevallos on this subject was submitted to the Senate with the message of December 21, 1804, probably in response to inquiries by Senators Bradley, Jackson, and Baldwin, who, it will be remembered had been appointed to consider the expediency of taking further action on the treaty. On the day following the receipt of the message and documents, this committee was discharged. Bradley immediately introduced a resolution that a select committee be appointed to consider and report "whether and, if any, what, further proceedings ought to be had by the Senate, in relation to the message on the disclosures made by the same."[3] This resolution was agreed to immediately after the Senate had advised the ratification of the treaty, and the three men

---

[1] *Am. State Papers, For. Rels.*, II. 605.
[2] *Ibid.*, p. 604 *et seq.*　　　　[3] *Sen. Exec. Jour.*, I. 461.

who had composed the earlier committee were appointed to this one.[1]

Towards the end of the session this committee brought in a report calling the attention of the Senate to the opinions expressed by the five lawyers. They stated their belief that the correspondence which these gentlemen had carried on with the agents of the Spanish government with an intent to influence the measures and conduct of the government of Spain, and to defeat the measures of the government of the United States, was in violation of the act of January 30, 1799.[2] The report concluded by recommending that the President be requested to lay before the Attorney General all documents relating to the matter and that if, in the opinion of the latter officer, the evidence was sufficient to warrant it the President be requested to instruct the proper officer to commence a prosecution under the act of 1799.[3]

Although the Senate never acted upon this report, the incident is an example of its tendency to take a high view of its prerogatives under the treaty-making power, and of its alertness to resent any action which might be in derogation of them. The Senate has always guarded well its constitutional powers, and more than once this attitude has been an important factor in its decisions concerning foreign affairs.

[1] *Sen. Exec. Jour.*, I. 463.

[2] A discussion of the origin of this act, known as the Logan Act, and of its subsequent history is to be found in Foster, *A Century of American Diplomacy*, pp. 226–231; see also McMaster, *History of the People*, III. 284.

[3] *Sen. Exec. Jour.*, I. 469–470.

The second point of interest in the procedure upon this convention is to be found in the use of the committee in its consideration. During the session of 1803 in which definite action was twice taken, only to be reconsidered, the Senate dealt with the matter directly. No committee was appointed. Before the subject was resumed in the following session, a committee of three was chosen, simply to ascertain the existing situation between the executive and the Spanish government with reference to the treaty. The functions of this committee ended with the communication by the President of this information. Acting directly the Senate then proceeded to pass the resolution of advice and consent, and, afterwards, appointed another committee to investigate the disclosures of interference by American lawyers. This course affords a typical example of the status of the committee in treaty affairs during this period, when no fixed rules regulated its use or function in the procedure of the Senate upon foreign relations.

THE SENATE AND THE LOUISIANA TREATY

In midsummer, 1803, President Jefferson issued a proclamation convening Congress in extraordinary session on the seventeenth of the following October to consider certain "great and weighty matters."[1] These matters concerned the treaties by which, on the thirtieth of the preceding April, France had ceded to the United States the vast territory of Louisiana. Congress was to be called upon to meet

---

[1] Richardson, *Messages*, I. 357.

the stipulated conditions and to provide for taking over and governing the empire which the executive had obtained.[1]

Following the usage which had become established by that time, the Senate on January 12, 1803, had approved the general proposition of a treaty with France on the question of our rights on the Mississippi, by confirming the nomination of ministers to carry on the negotiation. The sort of treaty which the Senate had provisionally sanctioned, however, was far different from that which subsequently was signed. Livingston and Monroe had been nominated "to enter into a treaty or convention with the First Consul of France for the purpose of enlarging and more effectually securing our rights and interests in the River Mississippi and in the Territories eastward thereof."[2] And their confirmation had been expressed in similar terms.[3] The treaty which was subsequently signed, however, was far different from that which the Senate had thus sanctioned. Consequently, so far as their previous action was concerned, they were now free to judge the question of ratification strictly upon its merits.

[1] Probably the most satisfying study of the diplomatic, constitutional, and political aspects of the Louisiana Purchase is to be found in Adams, *History of the United States*, II. ii–vi. Reference also has been made to McMaster, *History of the People*, II. xiii, III. xiv; Hosmer, *History of the Louisiana Purchase*, Ch. IX; Ogg, *The Opening of the Mississippi*, Chs. XI, XII. Channing, *The Jeffersonian System*, Ch. V. Moore, *International Law Digest*, Vol. V., Sec. 821, gives an excellent discussion of the diplomatic phase of the purchase, but does not treat the matter in its constitutional aspects.

[2] Richardson, *Messages*, I. 351.   [3] *Sen. Exec. Jour.*, I. 436.

After summoning Congress to meet and take such action as the situation demanded, Jefferson spent the remaining summer months in trying to work out the course to be recommended to them when they should come together. In this problem the time element was all-important. It was, indeed, the determining factor in the action not only of the President, but also of the Senate, and of the House of Representatives in the conclusion of the great purchase. All concerned would have given much to have weighed, considered, debated the issues involved, and finally to have secured the western empire in a manner and under conditions which squared with the political principles which the great majority of them had enunciated for years. But they feared that if the bargain were not sealed and the consideration- passed at once the other party might withdraw, or perhaps might not be able to deliver what had been promised; and in the crisis all three either altered or ignored their principles, and closed the transaction with a speed which would seem to disprove the familiar statement that under our form of government prompt and positive action in treaty-making can never be secured. In fact, the Senate ratified the treaty as it stood and Congress passed the measures necessary to give it effect in a shorter time than had been required for the President to make up his mind as to what action he should recommend to them.

In Jefferson's correspondence upon the proper course to be pursued in the dilemma in which he found himself little seems to have been said about the possibility of the rejection of the treaty by the Senate. That rejection was not impossible, however, was suggested to the President by his friend, Wilson Carey Nicholas, Senator from Virginia. After urging the President to keep his ideas concerning the unconstitutionality of the treaty to himself, he added, "I should think it very probable if the treaty should be declared by you to exceed the constitutional authority of the treaty-making power, it would be rejected by the Senate. . . ." [1] As few men were more closely in touch with the Republican majority in the Senate of 1803 than Nicholas this danger may have been real. At any rate, the advice was followed.

By the end of September the President had formulated the outline of his message to Congress. One proposal in the draft which he submitted to the members of his cabinet gave rise to an interesting discussion on the propriety of submitting a treaty to the House before the Senate had acted upon it. In order to complete the purchase as speedily as possible, Jefferson had indicated his intention of laying the treaties before both Houses of Congress at once. On October 1, Madison returned the President's notes upon the draft message, recommending that this section be altered to read, "These stipulations (instruments) will immediately be laid before the Senate, and if sanctioned by its concurrence will without delay be communicated to the House of Reps. . . ." Such a modification, Madison continued,

---

[1] Nicholas to Jefferson, September 2, 1803. Adams, *History of the United States*, II. 88, citing Jefferson Mss.

will also avoid what the theory of our constitution does not seem to have met [meant], the influence of deliberations and anticipations of the H. of Reps. on a Treaty depending in the Senate. It is not conceived that the course here suggested can produce much delay, since the terms of the treaty being sufficiently known, the mind of the House can be preparing itself for the requisite provisions. Delay would be more likely to arise from the novelty and doubtfulness of a communication in the first instance, of a treaty negotiated by the executive, to both Houses for their respective deliberations.[1]

Gallatin took practically the same position in the remarks on the proposed message which he handed to the President four days later. He observed:

It seems to me that the treaty ought not be laid before both Houses of Congress until after ratification by Senate. The rights of Congress in its legislative capacity do not extend to making treaties, but only to giving or refusing their sanction to those conditions which come within the powers granted by the Constitution to Congress. The House of Representatives neither can nor ought to act on the treaty until after it is a treaty; and if that be true no time will be gained by an earlier communication to that body. In asserting the rights of the House, great care should be taken to do nothing which might be represented as countenancing any idea of encroachment of the constitutional rights of the Senate. If, in order to be able to carry on a negotiation, the Executive wants a previous grant of money or other legislative act, as in the Algerine treaty, some Indian tribes, and last session (2) two millions appropriation, an application may be necessary before the negotiation is opened or the treaty held; but when as in the present case, the negotiation has been already closed and the treaty signed, no necessity exists to consult or communicate to the House until the

[1] *Writings of Thomas Jefferson* (Ford ed.), VIII. 266n.

instrument shall have been completed by the Senate, and President's ratification: in this instance there is no apparent object for the communication but a supposition that they may act, or, in other words, express their opinion and give their advice on the inchoate instrument, which is at that very time constitutionally before the Senate.[1]

A comparison of the two opinions shows that both secretaries based their objections to a simultaneous communication of the treaties to both Houses upon two main grounds. The first is one of principle — it ought not to be done. Madison states this most clearly when he says that the theory of the Constitution does not seem to have intended that the deliberations of the Senate upon an unratified treaty should be influenced by its discussion in the House. He might have gone farther and pointed out that submission to the larger chamber probably would be the equivalent of publication. In this event the Senate would be subjected to influence not only from the House but from the people as well. That the application of such influence would very seriously curtail, if not practically destroy the power of the Senate to decide independently the question of ratification is obvious. This conclusion doubtless led to the second objection to Jefferson's proposal which was one of expediency. Madison and Gallatin agreed that the innovation at this time would tend to delay rather than to expedite action. Probably both statesmen were confident that the Senate would resist any such encroachment upon its constitutional powers and feared that such resistance might delay and possibly

[1] *Writings of Albert Gallatin* (ed. Henry Adams), I. 154–156.

jeopardize the passage of the resolution of advice and consent to ratification. Jefferson decided to follow their advice in the matter and the treaties were not laid before the House until after they had been ratified.

When Congress met on October 17, the President, in announcing the signature of the treaties in his message to both Houses, said, "When these shall have received the constitutional sanction of the Senate, they will without delay be communicated to the Representatives also for the exercise of their functions as to those conditions which are within the powers vested by the Constitution in Congress." The treaties were at once communicated to the Senate. The message stated that the ratification of the First Consul was in the hands of his Chargé d'Affaires here, to be exchanged "whensoever, before the 30th instant, it should be in readiness." Three days later advice and consent to ratification was given by a vote of 24 to 7. The promptness of this action undoubtedly is to be attributed to the presence of an overwhelming Republican majority under the thorough control of the administration. Little is known of the debates during these three days, but it is likely that in the main they were along the same lines that were followed during the later discussion of the measures for putting the treaty into effect.[1]

From the standpoint of a study of the treaty-making powers of the Senate, however, perhaps the most interesting action in connection with the Louisiana treaty was taken after the adoption of the resolu-

[1] *Sen. Exec. Jour.*, I. 449–450.

tion of advice and consent. In public discussion the constitutionality of the treaty had been attacked upon two grounds. First it was declared that the President and the Senate had no authority to acquire Louisiana by treaty; secondly, that part of the treaty which provided for the future incorporation of the territory into the union was declared to be even more obviously beyond the powers of the treaty-making part of the government. No sooner had the Republican members of the Senate procured the agreement of the chamber to ratification than the following resolution was introduced by Pierce Butler, Federalist member from South Carolina: [1]

Resolved, That the President of the United States be requested to obtain from the French Republic, such a modification of the 3d article of the treaty, as will leave the government of the United States at liberty to make such future arrangements, or disposition of the territory of Louisiana, as, in their wisdom, may best promote the general interest; always securing to the free inhabitants of Louisiana, protection in their persons, security in their property, and the free and open enjoyment of their religion. [2]

The object of the desired modification was, of course, to release the nation from its pledge to incorporate the inhabitants of the ceded territory into the union. Had it been secured one of the two

---

[1] Under date of October 28, John Quincy Adams recorded in his diary, "Attended in Senate. Mr. Butler's resolution for a *further* negotiation with France, under consideration, debated until past three p.m., when we adjourned." *Memoirs of John Quincy Adams,* I. 268. Also on November 4 he noted that, "Mr. Butler's proposed resolution for a new negotiation with France was resumed and negatived." *Ibid.,* I. 271.

[2] *Sen. Exec. Jour.,* I. 450.

great constitutional objections to the treaty would have been obviated. The proposition was debated on the twenty-first and the twenty-second. On the twenty-first, however, the President had ratified the treaties and had exchanged his ratification for that of the First Consul. Saturday the twenty-second, the completed instruments were laid before both Houses with a request for legislation to make them effective.[1] When the Senate met again on Monday it declined to resume consideration of the Federalist resolution[2] and proceeded to provide the legislation which the President had asked for.

On Friday, the twenty-eighth, the Senate bill to enable the President to take possession of the ceded territory having been passed, and the House bill appropriating funds to pay for it not having been sent up, debate on Butler's motion of the twentieth was resumed.[3] Following this, the Senate debated the purchase appropriation bill from the House until November 3, when the measure was agreed to.[4] Thus, in its legislative capacity, the Senate had done what was necessary to put the treaty into effect. It then immediately went into executive session for the consideration of the resolution advising the President to attempt to secure a modification of Article 3. This proposal had support from both sides of the house. But when it came to a vote it was defeated 9 to 22, four Federalists and five Republicans being found in the affirmative.[5]

---

[1] *Annals of Congress*, 1803–1804, pp. 17–18.
[2] *Sen. Exec. Jour.*, I. 451.
[3] *Sen. Exec. Jour.*, I. 451; *Annals of Congress*, 1803–1804, p. 27.
[4] *Annals of Congress*, 1803–1804, p. 75.   [5] *Ibid.*, p. 452.

Very little reference to this proposal is to be found in the correspondence of the men involved. It seems obvious that the resolution never had a chance of adoption; and had the Senate presented it to the President, the latter would have been free to follow or to ignore the suggestion. It is clear, however, that the request was a perfectly proper one to be made by the Senate. That it was proposed, seriously debated, and supported by members from both parties is another interesting example of the fact that the Senate has always felt that it is as much within its constitutional powers to suggest the initiation of a negotiation as to pass upon a treaty already consummated by the executive.

THE KING–HAWKESBURY CONVENTION

The King-Hawkesbury Convention of May 12, 1803, was the first treaty to be lost by the refusal of the other signatory to accept an amendment proposed by the United States Senate. This convention provided for the fixing of the northeastern and northwestern boundaries between the United States and British territory.[1] That part of the northwest boundary between the Lake of the Woods and the Mississippi had been described by the second article of the treaty of 1783 as running due west from the most northwestern point of the lake to the river. Subsequently it was discovered that such a line would not intersect the Mississippi. The fifth article of the convention signed by Rufus King

---

[1] The northwestern boundary question is treated in Reeves, *American Diplomacy Under Tyler and Folk*, Ch. VIII.

and Lord Hawkesbury rectified the error by stipu-
lating that the boundary in this quarter should be
the shortest line which could be drawn from the
northwest point of the Lake of the Woods to the
nearest source of the Mississippi. It was provided,
too, that at the request of either party commissioners should be appointed to determine these
points and to run the line.[1]

This convention was laid before the Senate on
October 24, four days after the passage of the
resolution advising the ratification of the treaties
by which Louisiana was acquired from France.[2]
The Senate seems to have become alarmed at once
over the possibility of our rights under the Louisiana purchase being prejudiced by the terms of the
fifth article of the convention with England. John
Quincy Adams records in his diary that on October
31, "Mr. S. Smith intimated that since the ratification of the Louisiana Treaty this one must not be
ratified at all." [3] When the matter was next discussed, Senator Wright objected to ratification because he feared possible interference between this
treaty and that containing the cession of Louisiana.[4] On November 15, the convention was re-

[1] The convention and the correspondence submitted to the
Senate, together with documents explaining the action of the Senate
in amending the treaty by striking out the fifth article are printed
in *Am. State Papers, For. Rels.*, II. 584–591.

[2] *Sen. Exec. Jour.*, I. 450–451. Two days before the treaty was
submitted to the Senate Madison wrote to the American ministers
in Paris, Madrid, and London expressing his confidence that the
Senate would concur in the ratification of the treaty. *Ms.* State
Department, U. S. Ministers, Instructions, XI. 153.

[3] *Memoirs of John Quincy Adams*, I. 269.

[4] *Ibid.*, p. 271.

ferred to a select committee composed of Adams,
Nicholas, and Wright.[1]

After its chairman had conferred with Madison,
personally [2] and by letter, the committee presented
the following report:

That, from the information they have obtained, they
are satisfied that the said treaty was drawn up by Mr.
King three weeks before the signature of the treaty with
the French Republic of the 30th of April, and signed by
Lord Hawkesbury, without the alteration of a word;
that it had, in the intention of our minister, no reference
whatever to the said treaty with the French Republic,
inasmuch as he had no knowledge of its existence. But,
Not having the means of ascertaining the precise northern
limits of Louisiana, as ceded to the United States, the
committee can give no opinion whether the line to be
drawn, by virtue of the third [sic] article of the treaty
with Great Britain, would interfere with the said northern
limits of Louisiana or not.[3]

Adams and most of his Federalist colleagues believed that in these circumstances the fifth article
could not be construed in derogation of any rights
which the United States obtained by the purchase
of Louisiana.[4] But the Republican majority did

[1] *Sen. Exec. Jour.*, I. 454.

[2] *Memoirs of John Quincy Adams*, I. 273, 274. On the seventeenth Adams recorded that he had called on Madison who did not
approve of the resolution for the conditional ratification of the treaty.

[3] *Am. State Papers, For. Rels*, II. 590; See *Life and Correspondence of Rufus King*, IV. xxii, for evidence that this convention was
signed without knowledge of the French treaties of April 30.

[4] On the question "Will the Senate advise and consent to the
ratification of the 5th article?" Adams, Bradley, Dayton, Hillhouse.
Olcott, Pickering, Plumer, Israel Smith, and Tracy voted yea.
Of these all were Federalist except Bradley, Olcott and Smith,
Samuel Wright of New Jersey was the only Federalist voting nay.
Sen. Exec. Jour., I. 463.

not care to run any risks in the matter, and on
February 9, 1804, the Senate voted, 22 to 9, to
strike the fifth article from the treaty. It was
then unanimously agreed to advise the ratification
of the convention with this amendment.[1]

Although the rejection of the article concerning
the northwestern boundary had not met with the
approval of Madison, he at once sent to James
Monroe, who had succeeded King at London, instructions to secure the exchange of ratifications
with the British government. In these instructions
Madison explained the action of the Senate and advanced four reasons which led him to think that
the British government would accept the alteration. First, inasmuch as at the time when the instructions were drawn up and the convention signed,
neither party was aware of the conclusion of the
treaties ceding Louisiana, it would be unreasonable
that this convention should operate to restrict ter-
ritorial rights gained by the United States from
France. Second, if the fifth article were expunged
the northern boundary of Louisiana would remain
the same in the hands of the United States as it
had been in the hands of France; and it might be
adjusted and established according to the same
principles which in that case would have been ap-
plicable. Third, there was reason to believe that
the boundary between Louisiana and the British
territory north of it actually had been fixed by
commissioners appointed under the Treaty of Ut-
recht, and that a line run in accordance with article
five would pass through territory which on both

[1] *Sen. Exec. Jour.*, I, 463–464.

sides of the line would belong to the United States. Fourth, the adjustment of this line would be left open for future negotiation — a situation which in the past Great Britain had seemed anxious to bring about.[1]

The receipt of these instructions was acknowledged by Monroe in April.[2] Not deeming it worth while, however, to press American concerns upon the declining Addington ministry, our minister took no steps to secure an exchange of ratifications until Addington had given way to Pitt, and Lord Harrowby had superseded Lord Hawkesbury in the Foreign Office. In the new Secretary of State for Foreign Affairs, Monroe had to deal with one who regarded the United States and its aspirations with intolerance, if not with contempt. Moreover, as has been the case with some other English officials of small caliber, Harrowby did not consider it worth while to conceal his feelings from the representative of the former British colony. In his criticism of the American government for ratifying the King-Hawkesbury convention with the exception of the fifth article he certainly did not confine himself to "diplomatic expressions," but used language which Monroe deemed to be "calculated to wound and irritate."

In a letter to Madison dated June 3, Monroe reported the position taken by Harrowby on the practice of the Senate in ratifying treaties with alterations, and gave an account of his interview on the subject. Monroe wrote:

[1] *Am. State Papers, For. Rels.*, III. 89–90.
[2] Monroe to Madison, April 26, 1804, *Writings of James Monroe*, IV. 170.

He censured in strong terms the practise into which we had fallen of ratifying treaties, with exceptions to parts of them, a practise which he termed new, unauthorized and not to be sanctioned. I replied that this was not the first example of the kind; that he must recollect one had been given in a transaction between our respective nations in their treaty of 1794; that in that case the proposition for a modification in that mode was well rec'd, and agreed to; that to make such a proposition was a proof of an existing friendship & a desire to preserve it; that a treaty was not obligatory 'till it was ratified, and, in fact was not one 'till then. He said that the doctrine was not so clear as I had stated it to be; that there were other opinions on it, and seemed to imply, tho' he did not state it, that an omission to ratify did an injury to the other party of a very serious kind.

Monroe then explained why the fifth article had been excepted from the ratification, after which Harrowby

observed with some degree of severity in the manner, in substance, as well as I recollect, that, having discovered since this treaty was formed, that you had ceded territory which you do not wish to part from, you are not disposed to ratify that article.

Monroe denied this and advanced the arguments set forth in his instructions. The Englishman, however, "repeated again the idea which he first expressed, implying strongly that we seemed desirous of getting rid of an article in finding that it did not suit us." [1]

---

[1] Monroe to Madison, June 3, 1804. *Am. State Papers, For. Rels.*, III. 92–94. It is only fair to add that on June 23 Monroe wrote that he had come to the conclusion that Harrowby's ill manners during the above described interview were due to a state of mind which he was in at the time and were the result of a momentary impulse rather evidence of an unfriendly policy towards the United States. Monroe to Madison, June 23, 1804, *Writings of James Monroe*, IV. 197 n.

Although this unfriendly and uncompromising attitude on the part of the British ministers made Monroe's task exceedingly disagreeable, he continued to urge an acceptance of the amended treaty. On September 1 in a long interview concerning the various points at issue between the two countries he repeated all of his arguments, and afterwards sent them in written form for submission to the cabinet.[1] But Harrowby and the ministry were not to be moved. Instructions addressed to Anthony Merry, British Minister at Washington, under the date of November 7, 1804, stated that his Majesty's government would at all times be ready to reopen the whole subject:

but they can never acquiesce in the precedent which in this as well as in a former instance the American government has attempted to establish, of agreeing to ratify such parts of a convention as they may select, and of

[1] *Writings of James Monroe*, IV. 245. Monroe to Madison, September 8, 1804. *Am. State Papers For. Rels.*, III. 95–98. Monroe reported his action at this time in the following words: "We then proceeded to examine the convention respecting the boundaries in the light in which the ratification presented it. On that subject also I omitted nothing which the documents in my possession enabled me to say; in aid of which I thought it advisable, a few days afterwards, to send to his Lordship a note explanatory of the motives which induced the President and the Senate to decline ratifying the fifth article. As the affair had become by that circumstance in some degree a delicate one, and as it was in its nature intricate, I thought it improper to let the explanation which I had given rest on the memory of a single individual. By committing it to paper, it might better be understood by Lord Harrowby and the.cabinet, to whom he will doubtless submit it." A copy of this paper was sent to Madison. It traces the history of the boundary line in question and explains why the fifth article of the convention was rendered nugatory by the cession of Louisiana.

rejecting other stipulations of it, formally agreed upon by a minister invested with full powers for that purpose.[1]

The matter of the boundary was not again pressed, however, until the Grenville ministry was formed in 1806. Monroe then outlined the situation to Charles James Fox as soon as that statesman had taken possession of the seals of the foreign office.[2] In February he submitted to Fox a review of the previous negotiations between himself, and Hawkesbury and Harrowby. In this document he reiterated the familiar arguments for the ratification of the boundaries convention minus the fifth article.[3] But the new ministry proved to be as reluctant to countenance this innovation in treaty-making as had been the old. Fox, to be sure, was more courteous — conciliatory was the word Monroe used — than his predecessor had been; [4] but the treaty was not ratified. In May, when Pinckney was sent to join Monroe in an effort to settle the differences between the two nations, the latter was given a special instruction with reference to this question. If the British government declined to ratify with the omission of the fifth article, and was willing to do so with a proviso "against any constructive

[1] Adams, *History of the United States*, II. 424. Reference to MS. British Archives. In October Monroe left London on a special mission to Madrid, after having left open for future negotiation this and other questions pending between England and the United States. Monroe to Madison, October 3, 1804. *Am. State Papers, For. Rels.*, III. 98–99.

[2] Monroe to Madison, February 12, 1806. *Ibid.*, pp. 112–3.

[3] Monroe to C. J. Fox, February 25, 1806. *Ibid.*, pp. 113–114.

[4] Monroe to Madison, March 11, 1806. *MS.* Department of State, England, 12, James Monroe.

effect of the Louisiana convention on the intention of the parties at the signature of the depending convention" he was to "concur in the alteration with a view to bring the subject in that form before the ratifying authority of the United States."[1] This proposition, however, probably never was presented to Fox, who was taken ill soon after the arrival of Pinckney in London.[2] After the unfortunate Monroe-Pinckney treaty had been signed negotiations were entered into for a supplemental convention relative to boundaries.[3] But the effort produced no settlement and the matter was reserved for future discussion.

The King-Hawkesbury convention, however, was now finally recognized by the United States to be impossible of perfection. The subsequent history of the boundary controversy suggests very forcibly that at this time England may have been glad of a legitimate excuse for not ratifying the convention which Hawkesbury had signed. The rejection by the Senate of Article 5 gave her such an excuse — one probably all the more appreciated because it enabled her to put the United States in the wrong in the matter. This was not the last occasion upon which the action of the United States Senate gave to another nation the opportunity to retire gracefully from an agreement which it had come to regret.

As has been said, the King-Hawkesbury conven-

---

[1] Madison to Monroe, May 15, 1806, *Am. State Papers For. Rels.* III. 119.

[2] *Ibid.*, pp. 128–132 *passim*.

[3] Monroe and Pinckney to Madison, April 25, 1807. *Ibid.*, p. 162.

tion was the first treaty to remain unperfected because the other party refused to acquiesce in a qualified ratification by the United States. Further, this is the only occasion upon which another government has ever declined to proceed with ratification for the simple reason that it refused to accept the principle, that on account of its constitutional system the United States should be allowed to modify in ratification a treaty signed by its ministers in accordance with their instructions. Lord Harrowby's remarks to Monroe on this subject were not marked by the depth of the scholar, the suavity of the diplomat, or the vision of the statesman. Undoubtedly, however, he spoke truly when he told the American minister that the practice into which his country had fallen of ratifying treaties with exceptions to parts of them was new and unauthorized.[1] It was new because, until the Constitution of the United States had given to the Senate a voice in treaty-making, the nations of the world had commonly granted to those parts of their governments which negotiated treaties, authority to ratify them; and with rare exceptions treaties were ratified as signed. It was unauthorized because by the then generally accepted rules of international law a sovereign was bound to ratify what his minister, acting under full powers and within his instructions, had agreed to. Failure to ratify without extremely cogent reasons for refusal might be considered as a grave breach of faith. When Harrowby intimated that "an omission to ratify did an injury

[1] See Moore, *International Law Digest*, V. 184–202, for thorough discussion of this point in international law.

to the other party of a very serious kind" he was only expressing the generally accepted doctrine of his time.

The United States, in fact, was introducing a new principle into the diplomatic practice of the world. She had made her treaties a part of the supreme law of the land and therefore had given to the upper chamber of her legislature a part in enacting them. She was a federal state and as such had given to the representatives of her component parts a voice in making the treaties which bound them. She was a democracy and as such had declined to entrust the superlatively important function of treaty-making to the executive alone. Thus the very terms of her being went far towards determining the manner in which her relations with the other members of the family of nations were to be carried on. But as she was the first of her kind, the pre-existing rules of international intercourse made no provision for her unique method of making treaties, and when the action of her Senate made it necessary for her executive either to offer to ratify a treaty with modifications or to decline ratification at all, this method brought her into conflict with the established order of things.

In these circumstances it was inevitable that, sooner or later, she would encounter a Lord Harrowby. For in this situation his Lordship occupied a position for which he was eminently fitted and which he doubtless would have been proud to fill — that of the champion of things as they are. Hence his declaration that the American practice not only was new and unauthorized, but was not to be sanctioned. In the case of the King-Hawkesbury convention the established order of things prevailed; the modified treaty never was perfected. But that which the British minister lacked the vision to see came to pass. Upon many later occasions Senate amendments to treaties were submitted to the other party to the agreements accompanied by lengthy explanations of the features of the governmental system of the United States which put it in the power of the Senate to compel such action. And in due time the world consented to deal with the United States in the manner made necessary by her form of government. To-day what British ministry [1] would attempt to force the United States, with her system of treaty-making, into the mold provided for those states which still perform this function of government under the ancient principles? Indeed, England and practically every other democracy have now provided some method by which the representatives of the people may have a voice in determining what manner of treaties shall be made. The success of the American experiment demonstrated the practicability of such a system, and paved the way for similar democratic developments in other nations.

JOHN QUINCY ADAMS AND THE TREATY OF 1805 WITH TRIPOLI

Although finally ratified without amendment, the treaty of peace, amity, and commerce concluded

---

[1] Henry Cabot Lodge's admirable essay, "The Treaty-making Powers of the Senate," was occasioned by such a misunderstanding on the part of Lord Lansdowne in 1901, however.

with Tripoli June 4, 1805, was before the Senate from December of that year until the following April, and was the subject of prolonged and acrimonious debate in that body.[1]   By their insatiable greed and unfailing bad faith, the piratical rulers of the Barbary states finally had convinced the government of the United States that one fight would be cheaper than continual blackmail — that it would cost less to win a peace than annually to buy one.   Consequently in the spring of 1805 practically every sea-going vessel in the American navy was in the Mediterranean, for the purpose of bringing to a successful conclusion the naval campaign which had been carried on for several years.   Pressure of the fleet, and fear of a band of adventurers under the leadership of William Eaton, an American soldier of fortune, and Hamet Caramalli, a rival claimant of the throne, finally brought the ruling Bashaw of Tripoli to the point of considering a permanent treaty of peace with the United States.   This treaty was signed by Tobias Lear, of unhallowed memory.   Although negotiated at the cannon's mouth it provided that the United States should pay a ransom of sixty thousand

[1] Our diplomatic relations with Tripoli and the other Barbary powers are traced in Lyman, *Diplomacy of the United States*, II. xiii; the various treaties and other original material are here printed. Gardner W. Allen, in *Our Navy and the Barbary Corsairs*, presents both the naval and diplomatic phases of the question.   Chapters VI to XV cover our relations with Tripoli during this period.   See also Adams, *History of the United States*, II. xviii; McMaster, *History of the People*, III. xviii; Schouler, *History of the United States*, II. vi; Hildreth, *History of the United States*, V (Vol. II; 2d series) xvii, xviii; Channing, *The Jeffersonian System*, Ch. III. Humphreys, *The Life of David Humphreys*, II. ix–xi.

dollars for the crew of the frigate *Philadelphia*.
Also it left Eaton and Caramalli, with their followers,
to shift for themselves under conditions which by
many were thought to be as disgraceful to the
United States as they were disastrous to those individuals. The treaty, to be sure, provided that
in case Caramalli withdrew from Tripoli, the reigning Bashaw should return to him his wife and children, who had been held as hostages. But the
faithless Lear on the same day had signed an agreement that this delivery need not be made for four
years. Neither the other Americans on the ground
nor the United States government was informed of
this act.[1]

The opposition to the ratification of Lear's
treaty seems to have rested upon three grounds.
The first two concerned the treaty itself: It was
deemed subversive of the honor and interests of
the United States for it to buy a peace when it
was in a position to secure one by force of arms;
furthermore, the stipulation that the wife and
children of Caramalli be returned to him not having
been fulfilled, many Senators were of the opinion
that until they were the treaty should not be ratified. If John Quincy Adams was correct in his
deductions, ratification was also opposed, or at
least its delay was advocated, because "the Mediterranean fund, of two and a half per cent additional
duty, was by the terms of the law to cease three
months after the ratification of the peace with
Tripoli." [2]

[1] *Sen. Exec. Jour.*, II. 38.
[2] *Memoirs of John Quincy Adams*, I. 434.

A study of the proceedings of the Senate with reference to this treaty discloses the extent to which personal feeling, party politics, and the activities of the Senate in its legislative capacity may determine its action upon treaties. When submitted, December 11, 1805, the treaty was referred to Smith of Maryland, Tracy of Connecticut, and Worthington of Ohio, who considered it a week and then reported a resolution of advice and consent to ratification.[1] A few days later Tracy, the minority member of the committee, submitted a resolution which reflected the feelings of those senators who were dissatisfied with the management of the entire matter. This resolution, which with slight alterations was adopted three days later, is quoted as introduced both because it indicates the nature of the opposition to the ratification of this treaty and because it is an excellent example of the wide range of information which the Senate has always felt it proper to demand from the executive:

Resolved, That the President of the United States be, and he is hereby, requested to cause to be laid before the Senate, the instructions which were given to Mr. Lear, the Consul General at Algiers, respecting the negotiations for the treaty with the Bey and Regency of Tripoli; which treaty is now before the Senate for their consideration; and, also, the correspondence of the naval commanders, Barron and Rodgers, and of Mr. Eaton, late Consul at Tunis, respecting the progress of the war with Tripoli, antecedent to the treaty, and respecting the negotiations for the same; and whether the wife and children of the brother of the reigning Bashaw of Tripoli, have been delivered up, pursuant to the stipulation in said treaty; and what steps have been taken to

[1] *Sen. Exec. Jour.*, II. 3, 4, 9.

carry the said stipulation into effect; and also, to lay before the Senate any other correspondence and information, which, in the President's opinion, may be useful to the Senate, in their deliberations upon said treaty.[1]

After a delay of two weeks Jefferson responded to the general demand for information in two messages on the subject. One was addressed to both Houses of Congress and was an explanation of the coöperation of the United States and Hamet Caramalli against Tripoli. It also laid before the legislature an application for assistance from our former ally, or shall we say coöperator, who at this time was finding it difficult to live as a sovereign prince upon a "pension of 150 cents per day." [2]

The other message was to the Senate in its executive capacity, and stated that so far as the papers which had been asked for were available they were laid before it.[3] The reading of these papers consumed the remainder of the session and occupied three hours on the day following.[4] After debate covering two days, on motion of Bradley of Vermont, both messages were referred to a select committee composed of Bradley, Wright, Baldwin of Georgia, Smith of Maryland, and Tracy of Connecticut. Of these Tracy was the only Federalist, while Bradley, Smith, and Baldwin were among the leaders of the Republicans in the Senate.[5]

[1] *Sen. Exec. Jour.*, II. 12.

[2] Caramalli's petition to the people of the United States, in Lyman, *Diplomacy of the United States*, II. 391, n.; *Annals of Congress*, 1805–1806, pp. 48–50.

[3] *Sen. Exec. Jour.*, II. 14.

[4] *Memoirs of John Quincy Adams*, I. 382–383.

[5] *Sen. Exec. Jour.*, II. 14–15.

If the actions of a body of men are any index to their sentiments, it is fairly evident that this committee doubted the sincerity of Jefferson's statement that he had laid before the Senate all papers which could assist them in passing judgment on the treaty and the claims of Caramalli. For on the twentieth they secured the passage of a resolution requesting him to transmit copies of eight particular documents, which they described in great detail.[1] Two weeks later the desired papers, or extracts therefrom, were submitted with a statement that the latter contained everything relating to the case of Caramalli to be found in the original documents.[2]

After this the treaty was discussed upon several occasions, but no further action was taken until Bradley of the committee brought in a resolution to postpone further consideration until next session; to request the President in the meantime to ascertain whether the wife and children of Hamet Bashaw had been delivered up to him, and if not, why not; and to cause this information to be laid before the Senate. The motion for this resolution was ordered to lie for consideration.[3]

In the meantime this same committee had been carefully considering the application of the abandoned coöperator. Three days later Bradley presented a report and a bill on the subject.[4] The

---

[1] *Sen. Exec. Jour.*, II., 17.   [2] *Ibid.*, p. 20.   [3] *Ibid.*, p. 28.

[4] Of the report Pickering wrote to Rufus King as follows: "It is drawn, substantially by Bradley, and agreed to by all of the comtee. (As Tracy tells me) except Baldwin." Pickering to King, March 21, 1806. *Life and Correspondence of Rufus King*, IV. 505.

report outlined the dealings of the American diplomatic and naval officials with Caramalli, presented his case as that of a much injured individual, and laid the burden of blame for the whole affair upon Tobias Lear.[1] The bill provided for substantial relief for the injured ex-Bashaw.

The bill came up for third reading on March 31.[2] During the several days of debate which followed, Adams bore the chief burden of battle in opposition to the bill and to the report of the committee. The objection seems to have been not so much to an appropriation for the relief of Caramalli as against the report which based his claim upon right and justice, and not upon the liberality and magnanimity of the United States. Adams also defended Lear in the course he had taken in concluding the treaty.[3]

[1] Lear, in fact, was censured both for abandoning the ex-Bashaw and General Eaton, and for agreeing to pay $60,000 for the American prisoners. The report severely criticized his course from beginning to end, and probably expressed with fair accuracy the disgust of a considerable number of Senators with the treaty and the method of its negotiation. *Annals of Congress*, 1805–1806, pp. 185–188.

[2] *Ibid.*, p. 210.

[3] Of his speech of April 1 against the bill Adams wrote, "The Invalid bill passed as amended by the committee of the Senate, with some little debate. I was unable to give it proper attention, being employed in preparing to meet the bill in favor of Hamet Caramalli. This was taken up soon after twelve o'clock. Mr. Bradley, the chairman of the committee which reported the bill, made a speech of about an hour and a half in support of the report accompanying the bill and in answer to my yesterday's objections and those of Mr. Baldwin. I replied in a speech of about the same length, and endeavored to prove, by recurrence to the documents, that the report was erroneous in all its parts." *Memoirs of John Quincy Adams*, I. 425. This speech was reported in *Annals of Congress*, 1805–1806, pp. 211–224. On April 2 Adams recorded

Adams and Sumter and those of their way of thinking seem to have had the better of the debate, for Sumter's motion to recommit the bill, report, and documents prevailed against stern opposition. The vote was 14 to 15, with four of the six Federalists present among those who supported Bradley and his committee.[1] A question then arose whether the reference was to the same committee or to a new one. The decision of the Senate was a final blow to the pride of Bradley and his friends, and apparently a source of considerable satisfaction to Adams, who that night made the following entry in his diary:

It was finally referred to the same [committee], with the addition of two new members — General Sumter and myself. S. Smith, who was on the former committee,

in his diary, "about one the bill in favor of Hamet Caramalli was again taken up, and Mr. Wright, in a speech of more than two hours, replied to my yesterday's objections. He abandoned, however, almost the whole ground taken by the committee, and placed the claim upon a foundation altogether different. Mr. Bradley began to propose amendments to his own bill. General Sumter opposed them, on the ground that the bill was connected with the report, which he *disapproved in all its parts.* Senate adjourned without a decision. Mr. Baldwin and Mr. Sumter came to me after adjournment, and consulted with me how we could dismiss the bill so as to show our dissent from the report and yet do something for the Tripolitan ex-Bashaw who, as all agree, has some claim upon our generosity. By agreement with them I agreed to call on Mr. Madison, who, from his knowledge of all the circumstances, might suggest something which we may adopt. I called on him accordingly this evening, and he appeared to be well pleased that something temporary, like what General Sumter has suggested, should be agreed to. He expressed himself with his usual caution, but with disapprobation of the report. . . . " *Memoirs of John Quincy Adams,* I. 426.

[1] *Annals of Congress,* 1805–1806, p. 225. *Memoirs of John Quincy Adams,* I. 427.

offered to excuse himself, being now President pro tem.; but Mr. Tracy, complaining that the *feelings* of the committee had been injured, urged Smith not to excuse himself. So that he agreed still to serve.[1]

The addition of these two gentlemen could hardly be expected to increase the harmony of the committee. Sessions were held on the fifth, the seventh and the ninth of April, and according to Adams's descriptions were marked by violence of language and bitterness of feeling. All of the members of the old committee but Wright are reported to have become extremely anxious to postpone the whole matter until the next session. Adams and his followers desired to withdraw both the bill and the report and to make mere temporary provision for Caramalli. When Adams was not in the Senate, or meeting with the committee, he seems to have been interviewing naval officers, or looking up records for evidence to support his contentions. But even John Quincy Adams did not have the gift of omnipresence, and on the ninth, while he was at the auditor's office examining the state of Mr. Eaton's accounts Bradley hurried through the Senate a resolution which postponed further consideration of the bill and the report until the first Monday of the following December.[2]

[1] *Memoirs of John Quincy Adams*, I. 427–428.
[2] Adams's explanation of how the accident occurred is worth reading. The entry for April 9 begins, "I called again this morning at the Auditor's office, to examine the state of Mr. Eaton's accounts, and obtained part of the information I want. This, however, delayed me so that I could not attend the committee on the bill in favor of Hamet Caramalli. I got to the Capitol about twenty minutes after the hour at which the Senate meets and found that

In the midst of this bitter fight in legislative sessions over the report on the negotiation and the treaty, and the bill for Caramalli's relief, the treaty itself was brought up again for consideration by the Senate in its executive capacity. It will be remembered that on March 14, three days before the introduction of the report on the claims of Caramalli, Bradley had introduced a resolution to postpone consideration of the treaty until the next session, and for other purposes. On April 7 consideration of this resolution was resumed.[1] As might be expected the proponents of the report were the opponents of the treaty. At this point appears the third ground for opposition to immediate ratification, for Adams reports Bradley to have finally made "the avowal that the two and a half per cent additional duty, which by law must cease three months after the proclamation of peace, is wanted for other purposes, and is a further inducement to postpone." [2]

On the following day the resolution to postpone was rejected, twenty to ten, "after a long and animated debate." Tracy and Wright were the only members of the committee who voted with Bradley on this question.[3] And yet Adams, always suspicious, still expected that the matter would be postponed. That night he wrote:

the committee had taken advantage of my absence to report a postponement of the subject until the next session, which the Senate had agreed to." *Memoirs of John Quincy Adams*, I. 432. Also *Annals of Congress*, 1805–1806, p. 231.

[1] *Sen. Exec. Jour.*, II. 31.

[2] *Memoirs of John Quincy Adams*, I. 431.

[3] *Ibid; Sen. Exec. Jour.*, II. 31.

Yet from the complexion of the votes, I think it will end in that. The *Presidential* votes were for postponement. I mean by this, the men who get in whispers his secret wishes, and vote accordingly. Hence I conclude the Treaty shall not be ratified. And the true reason is to avoid the discontinuance of the two and a half per cent.[1]

Bradley's resources, indeed, had not been exhausted with the defeat of his motion to postpone. Its rejection was followed by an unsuccessful attempt to make ratification contingent upon the delivery of the ex-Bashaw in accordance with the third article of the treaty.[2] On the twelfth, however, the proposed amendment was voted down, and in the face of opposition at every step the resolution to advise and consent to the ratification of the treaty as signed was passed, 21 to 8.[3]

Adams's final comments on the proceedings reveal the tenseness of the struggle. He wrote:

Precisely at twelve I moved to go upon executive business, and the Treaty with Tripoli was taken up. Mr. Bradley, who had obtained leave of absence after Monday next, went away last night. Mr. Wright's amendment, to make the ratification conditional on the delivery of Hamet's wife and children, was first debated, and rejected, twenty to nine. Mr. Smith of Ohio then moved a postponement to the first Tuesday in December next; and just at six o'clock P.M. the question on the ratification was taken and passed — twenty-one to eight. The debate was very warm, zealous and vehement — General Sumter and myself in favor of the ratification; Messrs. Wright, Adair, White, Smith of Ohio, Tracy, and Pickering against it. The speeches of these gentle-

---

[1] *Memoirs of John Quincy Adams*, I. 431.
[2] *Sen. Exec. Jour.*, II. 31.   [3] *Ibid.*, pp. 31–32.

men, excepting Smith and Tracy, were as much *at* me as
to the questions in discussion; to Mr. Tracy and Mr.
Pickering I made no reply. It was seven in the evening
before I got home.[1]

On the nineteenth Adams again expressed his con-
viction that the desire to continue in operation the
law providing for the "Mediterranean fund" was
the real reason for the opposition to ratification.
He wrote,

The Mediterranean fund, or two and a half per cent.
additional duty, was by the terms of the law to cease
three months after the ratification of the peace with
Tripoli. This was the principal *real* obstacle to the ratification, but did not eventually prevail. We advised
the ratification last Saturday.[2]

There seems to be no additional evidence to show
that Adams was justified in his belief that the
desire to continue this augmented duty was at the
bottom of the opposition to the treaty. Certainly
it is hard to believe that Jefferson was secretly in-
triguing for its defeat. The sixty thousand dollars
had been paid; the American fleet in the Mediterranean had been greatly reduced and the failure
of the treaty almost certainly would have caused
the administration much additional expense and
anxiety at a time when all of its energy and resources were needed in other directions; Jefferson
was the last man to fight any one on a question of
national "honor" and would have preferred to have
had his navy "hauled up" than on the high seas.
But whether Adams was totally or only partially
wrong in his surmises there seems to be little ques-

[1] *Memoirs of John Quincy Adams*, I. 433.   [2] *Ibid.*, p. 435.

tion that the treaty owed its ratification in large part to his activity — a fact which did not improve the already strained relations between him and his party. After the ratification of the treaty Adams brought in a bill for the temporary relief of Hamet Caramalli which passed before the end of the session.[1]

The Tripolitan treaty of 1805 was the last treaty to be considered by the Senate for a period of almost ten years. It has been deemed worth while to trace in detail the action of the Senate upon it because it illustrates the operation of the treaty-making power of the Senate as it was then exercised, and because it also gives some idea of the complex forces that work for or against even the most simple treaty when it is before the upper house.

[1] *Annals of Congress,* 1805–1806, pp. 242, 244, 246, 1106.

CHAPTER VIII

The Genesis of the Senate Committee on Foreign Relations

BETWEEN December, 1805, and February, 1815, no treaty was laid before the United States Senate for its constitutional action. Yet there are few periods in the history of this country during which its relations with the governments of Europe played a greater part in the political, social, and economic life of the people, or exercised a more potent influence on the destiny of the nation. For ten years preceding the Treaty of Ghent, at every session of Congress a large proportion of the most important business transacted had to do with French decrees and British orders in council, with impressment, with Spanish aggressions on the southern border with the Barbary corsairs, with embargoes, with enforcement acts, with the privileges of foreign ministers, with the maintenance of neutrality, with wars and rumors of wars. Domestic politics turned on foreign issues; the greatest men in both parties gave to foreign affairs their first thought and their gravest attention. It was during this decade, as crowded with diplomatic strivings and international activity as it was devoid of international agreements, that the Committee on Foreign Relations of the United States Senate came into being.

The antecedents of the committee, however, must be sought in the records of the earliest years of government under the Constitution.[1] The practice of referring the business of treaty-making to select committees began with the reception of the first Presidential message on the subject. During Washington's administrations, however, there was no standing rule providing for such reference, and committees were used when and as the Senate saw fit — as the convenience of the moment dictated. But even in these circumstances there appears to have been a strong tendency to concentrate responsibility in treaty affairs in the hands of a few men. During the first eight years of the government eighteen treaties with Indian tribes and foreign nations [2] were submitted to the Senate for its advice and consent to ratification, and its advice was sought in the interpretation of one other treaty. In the consideration of these nineteen treaties the Senate employed nineteen committees, to which

[1] McConachie, *Congressional Committees, A Study of the Origins and Development of our National and Local Legislative Methods*, devotes Chapters VIII and IX to the committee system of the Senate. The first of these discusses sectionalism as it has been manifested in the committee, the several methods by which committees have been chosen, and the relation of the system to political parties. The second, entitled "Interior Organization," treats of procedure, majority and minority representation, the organization of the committees themselves and their relation to the business of the Senate. Very little attempt is made to trace historically the rise of the committee system or of any one committee. Harlow, *The History of Legislative Methods for the Period Before* 1825, Chs. XII. and XIII. traces the development of the Standing Committees of the House of Representatives.

[2] This includes additional articles upon which the Senate took separate action.

were referred questions connected with the negotiation, ratification, or interpretation of eleven different treaties. The total membership of these
nineteen committees was sixty-eight, while sixty-six
individuals served in the Senate during these years.
Yet these sixty-eight committee places were filled
by just twenty-four Senators; that is, two more
than a third of the Senate membership did all of
the committee work on foreign and Indian treaties.

Nor do these figures tell the whole story of specialization and concentration of power in this field. Of
the twenty-four Senators who served on these committees, five held more than half of the sixty-eight
places. These five were the most powerful Federalist members of the upper house. Caleb Strong
served on nine committees, Robert Morris on eight,
Rufus King and Oliver Ellsworth on seven each,
and George Cabot on four. Nor is the situation
altered when only those committees which acted
upon treaties with foreign nations are considered.
There were ten such committees, whose membership totaled forty-two, and upon which sixteen different individuals served. The five Federalist
friends whose names have been mentioned held
twenty-six of these forty-two places. In addition
they were primarily responsible for the Jay Treaty
from the conception of the idea to the ratification
of the completed instrument — and this despite the
fact that the Senate appointed no committee on
this matter.

These facts would seem to lead to the conclusion
that during Washington's administrations there was
a comparatively small group of members to whom

the Senate regularly intrusted a large part of the work which devolved upon it in the performance of its treaty-making functions, and to whom it habitually looked for guidance in this field. It is evident, however, that it did so not in accordance with any rule or fixed precedent, perhaps not even consciously, but simply because this was the easiest method of transacting this sort of business. It was only through succeeding years that the Senate established a standing committee which assisted it in the consideration of all problems of foreign affairs in accordance with a regular procedure.

In further tracing the development of this committee, attention must be given not so much to the activities of the Senate in the negotiation and ratification of treaties, as to the manner in which the upper house performed its more genuinely legislative functions. During the first twenty-five years of its existence it considered measures having to do with foreign affairs more frequently in legislative than in executive session. And it is an interesting fact that the Foreign Relations Committee, which to-day is usually thought of as a committee primarily for the consideration of treaties, really grew directly out of the legislative rather than the executive activities of the Senate.[1]

---

[1] It should be noted that during the whole of the period under consideration Senate committees were chosen by ballot, a plurality of votes electing. In December, 1805, John Quincy Adams observed, in his diary: "As our committees are all chosen by ballot the influence and weight of a member can very well be measured by the number and importance of those of which he is a member." He added, "In this respect I have no excitements of vanity." *Memoirs of John Quincy Adams*, I. 329.

As has been indicated in the case of treaties, in no sense was there a standing committee to which all business involving foreign relations was regularly referred. In many instances important matters of this sort were acted upon by the Senate without the assistance of any committee, and lengthy and weighty communications from the Executive explaining the labors of our diplomatic representatives abroad frequently were read and discussed on the floor without any suggestion that they be referred to any smaller body of Senators. Frequently select committees were raised to consider particular problems, and with rare exceptions they went out of existence with the solution of those problems. In a few instances, however, such a committee might be continued throughout a session, either because the business referred to it was not more quickly concluded, or because new references of matters more or less germane to the original subject were made to it from time to time. It is in these exceptional instances that are to be found the earliest steps in the evolution from the temporary, select committee on some specific question, to the standing committee on foreign relations to which all business concerning foreign affairs invariably was referred.

The first committee of this exceptional character existed during the third session of the first Congress. In his annual message, delivered December 8, 1790, Washington called the attention of Congress to the distressed condition of American commerce in the Mediterranean, and recommended that measures be devised for its relief and protection.[1] A week

[1] *Annals of Congress*, 1789–1791, II. 1730.

later the Senate ordered that "Messrs. Langdon, Morris, King, Strong, and Ellsworth be a committee to consider that part of the President's speech which refers to the commerce of the Mediterranean." [1] The form of this order is worthy of note, because it was in this manner that the Senate in later years raised the committees which developed into the Committee on Foreign Relations. In fact, the entire standing committee system of the Senate grew out of the reference of particular parts of the annual messages to select committees. This practice, however, did not become general until after 1797.

The particular committee here under discussion continued in active existence throughout the session, and possessed a greater number of the characteristics of the later standing committees than did any committee raised for ten years afterwards. To it was entrusted all of the business concerning American captives in Algiers, the protection of American trade in the Mediterranean, and our commercial treaty with Morocco.[2] Each matter was referred as it arose, and the Senate usually named the committee as that "appointed on the 15th day of December to consider that part of the President's Speech which relates to the commerce of the Mediterranean."

At the beginning of the next session of Congress six committees were appointed to consider particular matters of business mentioned in the President's

[1] *Annals of Congress*, 1789–1791, p. 1735.
[2] *Ibid.*, pp. 1740–1741; 1744, 1749, 1753, 1763, 1773–1776; *Compilation of Reports, Sen. Com. For. Rels.*, IV., 5–6; *Sen. Exec. Jour.*, I. 72, 78.

address, but with the possible exception of one on consuls and vice-consuls, none of these had to do with treaties or foreign relations.[1] Shortly afterwards, however, a petition asking that Congress reimburse private individuals who had ransomed an American captive at Algiers was referred to a committee with the same personnel as the Algerine committee of the preceding session, except that Butler was substituted for Ellsworth. During the remainder of the session all business pertaining to Algiers was referred to this group.[2] At the same time, however, other matters concerning our relations with foreign nations were referred to other select committees, so that in neither session did there exist a body which with any degree of accuracy could be called a committee on foreign relations.

The non-existence during this period of any such committee may be admirably illustrated by a recurrence to the proceedings of the Senate during the first session of the third Congress. During this session of 1793–1794 the situation was tense between the United States and France, England, and Spain, and much of the time of Congress was occupied with foreign affairs. On December 5, 1793, Washington communicated a message with a great mass of papers upon French-British-American relations. These were soon followed by a similar communication upon Spanish affairs. On January 15 additional papers revealing the situation between the United States and France were sent in, and on the

---

[1] *Annals of Congress,* 1791–1793, pp. 24–25.

[2] *Ibid.,* pp. 26, 29, 41; *Compilation of Reports, Sen. Com. For. Rels.,* VIII. 6; *Sen. Exec. Jour.,* I. 91.

day following a message with further documents touching the same subject. A week later extensive extracts from the dispatches of our minister at London were given to Congress, and on the next day the Senate passed a resolution requesting Washington to lay before it the correspondence of our minister at Paris with the French Government and with the Department of State. During February, March, and April other communications on foreign relations were received from the President. Yet not one of these messages was referred to a committee, and during the entire session only two committees were raised that had anything to do with foreign affairs.[1]

During the administration of John Adams little conscious progress was made in the development of a standing committee on foreign relations. Possibly for the very reason that during these years the attitude of the United States toward France, England, and Spain was the paramount, or at least the most spectacular issue of national politics, the Senate preferred to act directly in foreign affairs. The nearest approach to a foreign relations committee was made during the long and momentous session which began on November 13, 1797. At the opening of the special session of the preceding summer Adams had recommended the strengthening of the navy as a measure of precaution against further trouble with France.[2] In his first annual

[1] *Annals of Congress*, 1793–1795, pp. 14–15, 19, 31, 32, 37, 38, 55, 56, 62, 80; *Am. State Papers, For. Rels.*, I. 141–243, 247–288, 309–311, 312–314, 315–323.

[2] Richardson, *Messages*, I. 233–239.

address he again urged that every exertion should be made for the protection of our commerce — and that the country should be placed in a suitable posture of defense.[1] Two weeks later the Senate ordered that "Messrs. Goodhue, Laurance, Tracy, Bingham, and Gunn, be a committee to take into consideration that part of the President's speech, which recommends some measures being adopted for the security and protection of the commerce of the United States; and to report thereon by bill or otherwise."[2] During the seven months of this session scarcely a day passed that these five men were not engaged in considering one or more measures having to do with, or arising out of our relations with France. Almost all of the measures of defense and offense that arose out of the French quarrel either originated with them or passed through their hands. To this committee was referred the message in which the President set forth the flagrant violations of American neutrality by the French privateer *Vertitude*, after that vessel had sunk a British merchantman in Charleston harbor. They received for consideration Adams's pessimistic communication of March 19 — which declared that there was small chance of our envoys accomplishing the objects of their mission, and recommended energetic measures of defense. In this committee originated the bills by which the Senate proposed to cope with the situation, and to them were referred also those measures which were sent up from the House. On June 21, 1798, they presented the

[1] Richardson, *Messages*, I. 250–254.
[2] *Annals of Congress*, 1797–1799, I. 475.

bill declaring the French treaties to be void and of no effect. All told, they reported eight Senate bills and received for consideration seven House bills concerning measures affecting our relations with France, each of which they piloted through its course in the Senate. In addition, they reported one resolution and considered two Presidential messages which were referred to them.[1]

Yet despite this activity, a careful study of the proceedings of the session reveals how far this group was from being a committee on foreign relations, or even on French affairs. It also demonstrates conclusively that at this time no such committee existed, or was considered to exist. Of the eight messages with which Adams laid before Congress the correspondence of our unfortunate envoys to France, and other documents of like nature, only two were referred to this committee. The other six were considered by the Senate as a whole, and not one of them was given to any committee. In most cases the message and accompanying documents were ordered to be printed, and then were acted upon directly by the Senate as it saw fit.[2]

It was almost at the end of Jefferson's second administration, during the memorable special session of 1807–1808, that the natural tendency of the Senate to follow the lead of a relatively small group of men in the transaction of a particular sort of

[1] *Annals of Congress,* 1797–1799, I. 497–498, 505–506, 523–525, 529, 540, 542–543, 548, 571–573, 585–586, 590–591, 597, 604, 609; *Am. State Papers, For. Rels.,* II. 116–119, 152.

[2] *Annals of Congress,* 1797–1799, I. 516, 517, 555, 571, 581, 585–586; *Am. State Paper*, *For. Rels.,* II. 150–151, 153–163, 169–182, 185–188, 188–199, 199–201.

business gave rise to a real, although not a recognized standing committee on foreign relations. During the session the following matters, dealing directly with British relations or with measures made necessary by them, were either referred to or reported from select committees: so much of the annual message as related to the recent outrages of British armed vessels within the jurisdiction of the United States, and to the legislative provisions which might be expedient as resulting from them; Jefferson's embargo message; the embargo bill; the enforcement act, sent up from the House; the House bill to continue the act to protect American commerce and seamen from the Barbary Powers; Jefferson's message submitting the British orders in council of November 11, 1807; the supplemental non-importation act from the House; a plan from the President for an increase in the army; the House bill supplementary to the embargo; the message submitting the papers concerning the Leopard-Chesapeake affair; the Monroe-Pinckney negotiation, and the correspondence upon the subject of the rejected treaty, and all of the correspondence with reference to the negotiations with France; the bill authorizing the President to suspend the embargo under certain conditions; a report reviewing the condition of our foreign relations and recommending a continuance of the existing policy; a supplementary embargo bill; and, finally, House amendments to this bill.[1]

An examination of these measures at once dis-

[1] *Annals of Congress*, 1807–1808, I. 19, 34, 50–53, 63–64, 78, 79, 104, 127, 151, 153, 173–174, 178, 186, 361–371, 378.

closes a certain unity in all of them; all are directed to a common purpose. It might be expected, then, that they would have been referred to one standing committee — say upon British relations and national defense. Or, they might have been divided into two groups, one including those bearing directly on British relations, and the other those having to do with measures of defense. As has been said, however, each was referred to a select committee raised on that one subject. But, and here is the interesting development, all of the eleven committees created were composed of a very small number of men — men who were leaders in the upper house. The extent to which this concentration of control was carried is indicated by an examination of the make-up of the committees. John Quincy Adams served upon every one of them, and was chairman of one; General Samuel Smith of Maryland upon ten of the eleven, and was chairman of seven; Anderson of Tennessee upon five, and was chairman of two; Bradley of Vermont upon five; Mitchell of New York, and Gregg of Pennsylvania upon three; Giles of Virginia upon two, and was chairman of one; and Gaillard, Sumter, Hillhouse, and Milledge upon one each. The forty-three committee places were held by just eleven men, and of the eleven four sat upon only one committee.

Thus, although formally the Senate appointed eleven select committees, each independent of the others, yet the sum total of these bodies in membership practically amounted to a standing committee of eleven members, or, if the four men serving on just one committee be eliminated, of seven. In this instance, as in many others to be found in the study of the procedure of legislative bodies, the fact preceded the form; the institution, a standing committee on foreign relations, was gradually coming into existence before it was formally recognized and named.

From 1807 on, the development of the committee took on a more obvious form. As has been intimated, it finally grew out of the custom of referring to select committees given subjects mentioned in the annual messages. Such a committee was raised on so much of Jefferson's last annual message as concerned our relations with the Barbary powers.[1] A year later Madison's message set forth the critical condition of the relations of this country with Great Britain and Spain, and with it the President submitted to Congress diplomatic correspondence showing the situation with reference to these nations.[2] On the day following its delivery, Giles, of Virginia, submitted the following resolution for consideration.[3]

Resolved, That so much of the message of the President of the United States as respects the relations existing between the United States and Great Britain and France, with the accompanying documents, be referred to a select committee, with instructions to examine the same and

[1] Annals of Congress, 10th Cong. 2d. Sess., 1808–1809 p. 19.

[2] Richardson, Messages, I. 473–477.

[3] William Branch Giles was one of the most prominent of the Republican Senators during this entire period. He played an influential rôle in the action of the Senate in foreign relations, and served upon many of the committees appointed on the subject. His career is traced carefully, but without inspiration in, Anderson, William Branch Giles: A Study in the Politics of Virginia and the Nation from 1790 to 1830 (Menasha, Wisconsin, 1914).

report thereon to the Senate; and that the committee have leave to report by bill, bills, or otherwise.[1]

The resolution was adopted by the Senate, and Giles, Pope, Bradley, Goodrich, Leib, Sumter, and Gilman were chosen to be the committee.[2] This committee, or its leaders, all through the session played a predominant part in the haphazard efforts of the politicians in the Senate at once to stave off a war with England and to safeguard American interests, so far as was consistent with economy, Republican principles, and their own personal political ambitions. It was this committee that reported Giles's famous resolution, verbally castigating His Britannic Majesty's minister, Francis James Jackson, for the imputations of bad faith which he had cast upon the government, and pledging to the executive the support of Congress in repelling his insolence. At the same time it brought in a bill to prevent the abuse of the privileges and immunities enjoyed by foreign ministers in the United States.[3] Early in January the message from the President recommending an increase in the army and the organization of the militia was referred to the same committee. A week later Giles reported for the committee a bill authorizing the President to man, fit out, and officer the frigates of the United States. In this connection the committee had carried on a correspondence with the Secretary of the Navy, which was now ordered to be printed. On the last

[1] *Annals of Congress*, 1808–1809, I. 478.

[2] *Ibid.*, pp. 478–479.

[3] *Annals of Congress*, 1808–1809, I. 481–482; see also Moore, *International Law Digest*, IV. 511–513.

day of the month Mr. German presented resolutions providing for convoys for American merchant-
men, and this proposition was referred to Giles's
committee. The non-intercourse bill, which came
up from the House and which was intended to replace the expiring embargo, was intrusted to another
group, while a House bill providing for the protection of Mediterranean commerce was passed
without any reference whatever.[1] But Giles and
his colleagues participated in the action of the
Senate upon these measures, and, indeed, the committee exercised a potent influence over the Senate
during this session in all matters pertaining to
England and France.

Early in the session commencing in December,
1810, again upon motion of Giles, the Senate adopted
a resolution in terms identical with the one of 1809
setting up a committee on so much of the annual
message as referred to the relations between the
United States, Great Britain, and France.[2] Giles,
Crawford, Anderson, Goodrich, and Pope were
chosen to serve, all except Goodrich being Republicans of national prominence. To these men
were referred petitions of individuals asking to be
relieved from some of the provisions of the Non-
intercourse Act.[3] As a matter of fact, however,
the committee was of slight consequence during
this session, because the absorbing subject of interest during the winter of 1810 was that of the
Floridas; and the measures by which the Senate
proposed to bring this territory under the control

[1] *Annals of Congress*, 1808–1809, I. 520, 526, 530–531, 550, 587.
[2] *Ibid.*, 1810–1811, p. 16.   [3] *Ibid.*, pp. 21, 250.

of the United States were referred to other committees. Upon so much of the President's message as concerned the occupation of West Florida was raised a committee composed of Giles, Pope, Anderson, Crawford, and Bradley.[1] This was done upon motion of Giles, and it is to be noticed that, except for the substitution of Bradley for Goodrich, the only Federalist in the other group, the two committees were identical. In response to a confidential message from Madison, the subject of East Florida was taken up in secret session. Three measures were passed in this connection: an act authorizing the President to take possession of the country, a resolution declaring to the world the position of the United States with reference to this territory, and a resolution ordering that these acts be not published without the direction of the President.[2] Three committees acted in the transaction of this business. The first was composed of Clay, Crawford, Bradley, Smith of Maryland, and Anderson; the second of Bayard, Crawford, and Clay; the third of Anderson, Crawford, Clay, Bradley, and Smith of Maryland.[3] It will be observed, of course, that the personnel of these committees and of the two earlier chosen was strictly limited. All five, in fact, were composed of a small group of the leading Republicans of the upper house. Yet

[1] *Annals of Congress*, 1810–1811, pp. 16–17.

[2] See Hildreth, *History of the United States*, III. (2d series), xxiii; Adams, *History of the United States*, V. xv; Chadwick, *Relations of the United States and Spain, Diplomacy*, Ch. VI. It was in connection with this matter that Pickering was censured by the Senate for reading confidential papers in open session.

[3] *Sen. Exec. Jour.*, II. 176, 182.

formally each group was a separate, independent, select committee, bearing no organic relation to any of the others.

Again, at the beginning of the session of 1811–1812, so much of the annual message as concerned the relations between the United States, France, and Great Britain was referred to a select committee. Giles, Crawford, Gregg, Franklin, Lloyd, and Pope were named, Giles being once more the chairman.[1] The committee which was appointed a year later marked in its title an advance towards the form which later became the accepted one. In his annual message of 1812, Madison had adverted to our relations with Great Britain, with whom we were at war, and with France, Denmark, Russia, Sweden and the Barbary States.[2] On the day following, four motions were submitted providing for the reference of four of the most important subjects treated in the message to as many select committees. The first resolution includes so much of the message as concerned "our relations with foreign powers, the Military Establishment of the United States and volunteers."[3] All four resolutions were adopted, and Franklin, Campbell of Tennessee, Taylor, Varnum, Howell, Robinson, and Worthington were chosen to serve on the first-named committee. This committee was active throughout the session, and exhibited more of the characteristics

[1] *Annals of Congress*, 1811–1812, pp. 15–17.

[2] *Ibid.*, 1812–1813, pp. 13–14.

[3] *Ibid.*, p. 17. The other subjects were: The naval establishment of the United States; American vessels which had arrived in the United States laden with British manufactures; the revision of the militia laws.

of a real committee on foreign relations than had any of its predecessors. Early in the session a communication from Madison concerning the attempt which had been made through Jonathan Russell to bring about a suspension of hostilities with Great Britain was referred to it as "the Committee on Foreign Relations." [1] A few days later another letter on the same subject was referred to the "committee who have under consideration so much of the message of the President of the United States, of the 4th instant, 'as concerns our relations with foreign Powers.'" This matter of nomenclature may be of little importance in itself, but it is not without interest to observe how the name of this great committee gradually came into use. During this and several sessions following, the title "Committee on Foreign Relations" frequently, in fact usually, was applied to the body appointed under the sort of resolution which has been described. On the other hand, the committee often was referred to in other ways — described, rather than named.

A review of the measures which came before the committee during this session reveals a slight increase in the specialization of its functions. It was occupied with fewer matters not bearing directly on foreign relations, and at the same time the Senate passed or considered a smaller number of measures in this particular field without consulting it.[2]

A conscious step towards the specialization of the

---

[1] *Annals of Congress*, 1811–1812, 19.

[2] *Ibid.*, pp. 18–19, 21, 27, 39, 94, 101, 104, 105, 112, 113, 115, 117, 121.

function of the committee was made when Congress met in May, 1813. On the day following the reading of Madison's message, a resolution was introduced providing that so much of it as concerned our relations with foreign Powers and the military establishment be referred to a select committee. At the same time it was moved that the part of the message relating to the naval establishment be referred to another committee. The next day, however, military affairs were separated from foreign relations, select committees being set up on each of the three subjects.[1] During this session, also, a still greater homogeneity is to be observed in the measures considered by the committee, practically all of the business arising from our troubles with Great Britain passing through its hands.[2] At the same time, however, a very important part of the business of the Senate in the field of foreign relations was being carried on with the assistance of other groups. Early in the session Madison submitted to the Senate the nominations of Gallatin, Adams, and Bayard as peace envoys, along with that of Jonathan Russell as minister to Sweden.[3] The nominations of Gallatin and Russell were opposed, largely from political motives, but in the former case for the ostensible reason that the position was incompatible with that of Secretary of the Treasury, and in the latter upon the ground that it was inexpedient at that time to send a minister to Sweden. A bitter struggle followed, which resulted in the

[1] *Annals of Congress*, 1813–1814, I, 18–19.
[2] *Ibid.*, pp. 25, 31, 36–39, 45, 47, 55, 59.
[3] *Sen. Exec. Jour.*, II. 347.

rejection of both names. The fact of interest is that in considering the nominations, and in carrying on its struggle with the President over them, the Senate acted through select committees, rather than through the group which had been appointed at the beginning of the session to consider foreign relations. Not only that, but a comparison of the personnel of these committees with that of the Foreign Relations Committee shows that the membership of the former contained by far the weightier Senators.[1] A few years later neither of these conditions would have existed.

During the second session of the thirteenth Congress, which met in December, 1813, the functions of the Committee on Foreign Relations possessed even greater unity, and were of larger importance than during previous years. An enumeration of the matters of business coming before it is, perhaps, the most effective means of setting forth its functions at this time. During the session it had under consideration the following measures: the message of the President recommending an embargo, a bill which it reported in response thereto, and the House embargo bill which ultimately became law; the bill, which it reported, prohibiting the importation of certain articles derived principally from Great Britain; Madison's message submitting to Congress the British rejection of Russian meditation, and Lord Castlereagh's offer to treat for peace directly; the message recommending the repeal of the embargo

---

[1] *Sen. Exec. Jour.*, II. 347, 352, 354, 395. Adams, *History of the United States*, VII. 59–64, presents a most interesting discussion of this struggle, its outcome, and its political significance.

and the extension of additional duties for a period of two years after the war; two petitions on this subject; the bill for the repeal of the Embargo Act; a proposal to pass an act prohibiting the exportation of sheep from the United States; a bill, which it reported but which failed to pass, prohibiting the exportation of specie, gold or silver coins, or bullion; bills providing for the more effectual enforcement of the Non-Importation Act, and for the return to their own districts of vessels detained in other districts under the terms of the Embargo Act, and, finally, numerous bills for the relief of individuals seeking exemption from pains and penalties incurred by alleged violations of the Non-Importation and other war acts.[1]

These measures comprise all of the more important matters of general business arising out of the foreign relations of the United States at this time. All had some bearing on the war with Great Britain, and all were legislative in their character. But during this session no business concerning our relations with any other power came before the Senate, except the appointment of foreign ministers. This subject, of course, was considered in executive session, and no committees were employed in connection with any diplomatic appointment passed upon at this time. Thus the Committee on Foreign Relations had practically a monopoly of the business transacted by the Senate within its field.

The special session commencing in September, 1814, offers three points of particular interest in

[1] *Annals of Congress*, 1813–1814, I. 549, 550, 551, 562, 565, 570, 601, 613.

the history of the committee. The first has to do with the manner of its choice. Madison's message, laying before Congress the facts of the military situation and the needs of the army, the navy, and the treasury, contained no suggestions on foreign relations which demanded the immediate attention of the Senate. Consequently the usual reference to a select committee of that part of the message which touched upon such relations was hardly in order, and at the beginning of the session no such committee was created.[1] On October 10, however, the President communicated to Congress letters from the American peace envoys, and four days later submitted the instructions under which they were acting. Whereupon the Senate passed a resolution that these documents, together with the several communications from the President since the beginning of the session, should be referred to a select committee. Bibb, Taylor, King, Brown, and Chase were chosen as the committee, and during the remainder of the session were usually referred to as the "Committee on Foreign Relations." As such they were the organ of the Senate for the transaction of the same sort of business that had been assigned to similar committees in years past.[2] Such a body might, perhaps, be described as a quasi-standing committee. It was not created as a

---

[1] Richardson, *Messages*, I. 547–551. The only parts of the message which were referred to select committees at this time were those concerning the militia and military affairs. *Annals of Congress*, 1814–1815, III. 16, 24, 27.

[2] *Ibid.*, pp. 24, 27, 164, 245–250, 260, 269, 270, 275, 278, 280, 294–297.

standing committee, and, so far as the formal action of the house went, it was on the same basis as any select committee. But in everything but name it certainly possessed the characteristics of the standing committee, even to that of continuity of membership from session to session.[1]

On the last day of the session Bibb's committee brought in a report which is of interest because it was the first of a type which frequently appears in the later history of the Committee on Foreign Relations. Soon after Congress had assembled, Madison had communicated to both houses correspondence which had passed between himself and Admiral Cochrane, in command of the British fleet on the American station, relative to the devastation which the British threatened to mete out to American coast towns in retaliation for wanton destruction alleged to have been committed by the American army in upper Canada.[2] The incident mentioned was the burning of York, which later was pointed to by the British as a justification for the destruction of the public buildings in Washington and other outrages of the same nature. The Senate referred the correspondence to the Committee on Foreign Relations, and just before adjournment the chair-

[1] Bibb, the chairman of this committee, and Taylor, Chase, and Brown had served on the Foreign Relations Committee of the preceding session. Also the committee had dropped back to five members, the size which it had had until the year before, when it had gone to seven. Rufus King was the only member of the new committee who had not served on its immediate predecessor — and no man then in the Senate was possessed of more experience in the field of foreign relations than King.

[2] *Am. State Papers, For. Rels.*, III. 693–695.

man of this body submitted a report giving the result of their inquiries, which, it was declared, manifested "to the world that the plea which had been advanced for the destruction of the American Capitol and the plunder of private property" was without foundation.[1] As an organ for the formulation of the opinion of the Senate upon matters concerning the foreign relations of the United States, the committee has produced some manifestoes which have been of far-reaching importance in the history of the nation. Although its report on the "retaliating system" as practiced by Great Britain during the War of 1812 does not rank as an important state paper, yet it is worth noting because it is the first product of this sort of activity on the part of the committee.

The third significant event of the special session of 1814 was the use of the Committee on Foreign Relations in executive session in connection with the proceedings on the Treaty of Ghent. The incident occurred two days after the Senate had consented to the ratification of the treaty, when a motion to remove the injunction of secrecy from the proceedings and to print the documents connected therewith was referred to the "Committee on Foreign Relations."[2] The reference marks the point at which this committee, after having come into being during a decade when no treaties were before the Senate, began to perform the functions which inevitably were to be assigned to it, and in the exercise of which it was to reach its greatest usefulness and

---

[1] *Am. State Papers, For. Rels.*, III. 294–296.

[2] *Sen. Exec. Jour.*, II. 621.

power. Hitherto it had been a legislative committee; it had been used almost exclusively for the transaction of legislative business; no allusion to it is to be found in the executive journal. From this time on, its most important business was to be transacted in executive session, and every treaty laid before the Senate was to be considered by it.

At the beginning of the session of 1815 the usual reference of the several parts. of the annual message was made, and it was not until a year later, December, 1816, that the Committee on Foreign Relations became the first standing committee of the United States Senate.[1] On the day following the reading of Madison's last annual address, Nathan Sanford of New York submitted thirteen resolutions, each referring a certain part of the message to a select committee, with leave to report by bill or otherwise. On the next day, however, Senator Barbour of Virginia introduced a resolution providing that it should be one of the rules of the Senate that eleven standing committees, which were named, should be appointed at each session. After discussion during several days, the resolution was passed on December 10, the Committee on Foreign Relations heading the list. Three days later Barbour, Mason, King, Dana, and Lacock were chosen to be members of the committee.[2]

[1] *Annals of Congress*, 1815–1816, pp. 19, 20. Committees were chosen to consider those parts of the message concerning foreign affairs, the militia, military affairs, naval affairs, finance and a uniform national currency, manufactures, roads and canals, and a national seminary of learning within the District of Columbia.

[2] *Annals of Congress*, 1816–1817, pp. 18–22, 30, 32. The other committees named were those on finance, commerce and manu-

Thus was established the Committee on Foreign Relations of the United States Senate. Along with the ten other committees made permanent at the same time, it had gradually come into existence during the decade and more of stress and strain which preceded the conclusion of the War of 1812. During the earlier years of the government, treaties and foreign affairs generally had been referred to select committees occasionally but in accordance with no particular rules of procedure. An increasing pressure of business, a pressure which became heavy during the war, demanded a greater efficiency of the Senate. The demand was met by a specialization of function — by the development of a system of standing committees which practically came into existence some time before it was formally made a part of the organization of the Senate. This specialization developed first in the field of foreign relations, and as at this time the business in this field was almost wholly legislative in its nature, the Committee on Foreign Relations developed as a legislative committee. With the consideration of the

factures, military affairs, the militia, naval affairs, public lands, claims, the judiciary, the post office and post roads, and pensions. All of the members of this first Standing Committee on Foreign Relations were leaders in the Senate and in the nation. Barbour was a member continuously from 1816 until 1824, the last session before he left the Senate to become Secretary of War. He was chairman in 1816, 1817, 1820, 1822, 1823, and 1824. Nathaniel Mason was a member of the committee for twelve years, and was thrice chairman. Except for one session, Rufus King served from 1815 to 1823. S. W. Dana served only during the session of 1816, while Abner Lacock was a member for three years. King and Dana were the Federalist members.

message and documents on the Treaty of Ghent its executive functions began, and it became the organ of the Senate for the transaction of executive as well as legislative business within the realm of foreign affairs.

CHAPTER IX

The Senate and Treaties at the End of the Formative Period

The procedure followed by the Senate in its action upon the Treaty of Ghent departs in no important particular from the norm which had become established by 1805. The struggle between Madison and the upper house over the appointment of Gallatin, and their differences upon the propriety of recess appointments which were not to fill constitutional "vacancies," concern the appointing more directly than the treaty-making powers of the Senate. In finally confirming the appointment of commissioners to negotiate treaties of peace and of commerce with England, a treaty of commerce with Russia, and one of commerce with Sweden, no formal effort was made by the Senate to ascertain in detail what it was proposed to embody in the agreements.[1]

When the Treaty of Ghent was laid before the Senate in February, 1814, that body accepted it with what may, perhaps, be described as eagerness. The instrument was submitted on the fifteenth, and the President's statement that, "the termination of hostilities depends upon the time of the

[1] *Sen. Exec. Jour.*, II. 346, 348, 349, 351, 353–355, 384, 388–390, 451–454.

ratification of the treaty by both parties,"[1] led the Senate to expedite its consideration. The message, the treaty, and the accompanying documents were read, and by unanimous consent the treaty was read a second time, after which General Smith introduced a resolution giving the advice and consent of the Senate to its ratification. Rufus King, however, interposed with a motion that the President be requested to lay before the Senate all the instructions given to the envoys, together with all correspondence and protocols connected with the negotiation which they had not previously received. The adoption of King's resolution held up further consideration of the treaty until the next day, when, upon the receipt of the documents asked for, the resolution of advice and consent was passed without further delay.[2]

During the first session of the fourteenth Congress the two treaties which were acted upon by the Senate were considered under procedure which seems to have changed from that provided for by the rules which had been adopted in 1801 only in the employment of the committee on foreign relations. In the first executive message of the session Madison submitted the commercial convention with Great Britain, which had been concluded the preceding July,[3] and the treaty of peace with Algiers, which had been signed at the end of June. Both of the treaties and the documents which had accompanied

---

[1] *Sen. Exec. Jour.*, II. 618–619. It seems not unlikely that the necessity of speedy action led the Senate to deal with the question directly, and without the assistance of a committee.

[2] *Ibid.*, pp. 619, 620.   [3] July 3, 1815.

them were ordered to be printed for the use of the Senate, under an injunction of secrecy — action which was almost invariably taken from this time on immediately after the receipt of a treaty by the Senate. On the following day the British treaty was referred to the committee on foreign relations, which shortly afterwards reported a resolution of advice and consent. With slight modification this resolution was adopted, only one Senator opposing ratification. The treaty of peace with Algiers was not formally referred to the committee on foreign relations, but the resolution providing for its ratification was introduced by Mr. Bibb, the chairman of that body, and was passed without opposition.[1]

The commercial convention with Sweden signed by Jonathan Russell on September 4, 1816, was submitted to the Senate early in December.[2] Procedure upon it followed the customary lines, although the Senate gave its consent to ratification, only upon the condition that three of the articles be expunged. After first reading, the convention was referred to the committee on foreign relations, of which James Barbour of Virginia was then chairman.[3] Two weeks later Barbour brought in a report recommending that the treaty be printed in both French and English, and that a letter from Russell to the Secretary of State respecting its negotiation also be printed.[4] After the Senate had

[1] *Sen. Exec. Jour.*, III. 3, 4, 6–8. On January 2, 1816, on motion of Bibb, the injunction of secrecy was removed from the proceedings of the Senate upon the treaties with Great Britain and Algiers. *Ibid.*, p. 14.

[2] *Sen. Exec. Jour.*, III. 60–61.   [3] *Ibid.*, p. 61.

[4] This report appears in *Compilation of Reports, Sen. Com. For.*

considered the treaty in committee of the whole upon several different days, Barbour introduced a resolution providing for its ratification with the exception of the third, fourth, and sixth articles. This resolution was adopted on the following day with only two votes registered in the negative.[1]

The procedure of the Senate in considering the four treaties which were before them in 1815 and 1816, thus followed very closely the lines which had been laid down during the first fifteen years of government under the Constitution, except in the use which was made of a standing committee on foreign relations. Nor has there been any radical change in Senate procedure since 1816.

THE SENATE AND THE NEGOTIATION OF TREATIES

During this same period an important principle which had been gradually developing with reference to another aspect of the treaty-making power became more firmly established. This was the principle that the Senate should not attempt to participate formally in treaty-making until after the process of negotiation had been completed. Washington and the earliest Senates had endeavored to apply a different theory, which the early treaties with Indian tribes had proved to be unworkable, and which had gradually been abandoned in practice, although never formally renounced.

The matter had been threshed out very thoroughly in 1806, when the President was asked to

Rels., VIII. 26, under the incorrect date of January 3, 1817. It was submitted January 3, 1816. Sen. Exec. Jour., III. 68.

[1] Ibid., pp. 72, 74–75, 77, 78.

take certain specific action with reference to British aggressions on American commerce. The debate was upon the question of the adoption of the following resolution, the second of three which had been introduced by a committee of which General Smith, John Quincy Adams, and Joseph Anderson were the leading members:

Resolved, That the President of the United States be requested to demand and insist upon the restoration of the property of their citizens, captured and condemned on the pretext of its being employed in a trade with the enemies of Great Britain, prohibited in time of peace; and upon the indemnification of such American citizens, for their losses and damages sustained by these captures and condemnations; and to enter upon such arrangements with the British Government, on this and all other differences subsisting between the two nations, and particularly respecting the impressment of American seamen, as may be consistent with the honor and interests of the United States, and manifest their earnest desire to obtain for themselves, and their citizens, by amicable negotiations, that justice to which they are entitled.[1]

In the debate which followed the introduction of this resolution, some of the ablest students of the Constitution and most influential Senators of the day expressed their opinions upon the advisability of attempting to outline in detail the terms to be insisted upon by the President in a negotiation with a foreign nation. All agreed that the Senate would be within its constitutional rights in passing the resolution, but great differences of opinion appeared as to the expediency of such action. The adoption of the resolution was opposed upon the

[1] *Annals of Congress*, 1805–1806, p. 91.

ground that it would be disrespectful and officious; [1] because by grouping together a number of separate propositions, each one of which might be difficult to attain, and requesting the President to "demand and insist" upon all of them, it gave him only the alternatives of disregarding the advice of the Senate or of failing to conclude any treaty at all; [2] and because the adoption of such a resolution would decrease the responsibility which the executive ought to feel for treaty-making. [3] Other members urged

[1] Smith of Vermont. *Annals of Congress,* 1805–1806, p. 95.

[2] Upon this point Worthington said, "It is not, sir, that I am opposed to demanding or insisting on our rights; but it is because I fear the resolution taken together will embarrass the executive in negotiating a treaty to settle our differences. . . . With so wide a field of negotiation, with so many important objects to accomplish, I submit it to the good sense of the Senate, whether it will be proper to tie up the hands of the Executive in the manner contemplated in the resolution." *Ibid.,* p. 105. Adair emphasized the same point, contrasting the general nature of the first resolution with the specific instructions given in the second, and declaring that the latter went too far. "It is circumscribing the powers of the President, and tying him down to a particular point. It is making that the *sine qua non,* the basis on which alone he is to treat; at least it is doing this so far as an opinion of the Senate, expressed in this way, can do it. . . . It has been well observed by the honorable member from Tennessee, that in forming commercial treaties of this kind, there will be various points to consider, and that it may not be necessary to contend for strict justice in every punctilio; arrangements or treaties, when there are existing differences to settle, must always be a bargain of compromise and forbearance; in one point we may give a little, that we may gain in another. So it may turn out in settling our disputes with Great Britain. Why, then, are we not satisfied with expressing our opinion on the great principle of right and leave it altogether with our Chief Magistrate to enter into and point out the details?" *Annals of Congress,* 1805–1806, pp. 106–107.

[3] Bayard stated this objection as follows: "Mr. President, if there be any objection to the resolution now before us, it is that it

the adoption of the resolution on the ground that, far from being an assumption of power by the Senate, it was both the right and the duty of that body to advise the President in this way;[1] on the ground that it would impress the government of Great Britain that the United States was a unit in demanding the redress asked for;[2] and because by

shelters the Executive Government from that responsibility as to its measures which properly ought to attach to it. The duty prescribed by the resolution is of an Executive nature, and the President is charged with the care of those interests for which the resolution provides. By prescribing a course of conduct to the Executive, we release that branch of government from responsibility as to the event, and take it upon ourselves." *Ibid.*, pp. 101–102.

[1] Anderson set forth this position in the following words: "Let us examine the language of the Constitution upon this point. The Constitution says that the President shall have power, by and with the advice and consent of the Senate, to make treaties. Now, I contend that the true meaning of this clause is, that the advice should precede the making of the treaty, and that it was couched in the language in which we find it, for the purpose of obtaining the opinion of the Senate as to the principles upon which the treaty should be made." He then went on to cite the practice during Washington's time, and to point out that on account of its inconvenience this mode of taking the advice of the Senate had since fallen into disuse. "But," he continued, "the latter practise cannot, or ought not, be considered as condemning the construction of which I conceive the Constitution is fairly susceptible. Because the construction given by the first President so immediately after the adoption of the Federal Constitution must be considered as proceeding from the true sense and correct opinion which he then entertained of the *respective rights* of the treaty-making power." *Ibid.*, pp. 96–97. Mitchell declared that "In questions touching our foreign relations, the Senators are declared by the Supreme law of the land to be the President's counsellors. In urgent and arduous cases it was not only allowable for them to exercise this right, but it was their duty to do so." *Ibid.*, pp. 100–101.

[2] Bayard favored the passage of the resolution for this reason. He said, "For my part, sir, I do not consider the resolution as intended in any degree for the President, but as designed for the

it the Senate was sharing the responsibility for the
course of the executive, and giving greater weight
to the President's action.[1]

These arguments include several of the chief
reasons which have always been advanced for and
against the general principle involved. It cannot
be said, however, that at this time the Senate expressed any definite opinion upon the abstract
merits of the question. The resolution, to be sure,
was adopted by a large majority, but this apparently was because the Republicans believed that
it would strengthen the President in meeting the
crisis of our relations with Great Britain. The incident, therefore, probably proves no more than
that the Senate believed that, constitutionally, it
possessed authority to participate in treaty-making
at any stage in the process.

Exactly the same point was brought to an issue
soon after the ratification of the Treaty of Ghent.
Immediately after the Senate had accepted the
treaty, Rufus King introduced a resolution which
provided that the Senate should "recommend to,

British Government. . . . I do not mean that we should be considered as offering an empty menace to the British cabinet, but a
demonstration of the union of different branches of our Government
in demanding satisfaction for the wrongs done us. Foreign Governments calculate much on our divisions, our union will disappoint
these calculations." *Ibid.*, p. 102.

[1] Smith of Ohio exclaimed, "What is the object of the resolution?
It is, that this branch of the legislature shall share the responsibility
of employing means to execute the measure proposed. This is
magnanimous, as it is voluntary on the part of the Senate, for
in adopting the resolution we attach a degree of responsibility to
ourselves in the effects to be produced." *Annals of Congress*, 1805–
1806, p. 110.

and advise, the President" to pursue negotiations with Great Britain for the purpose of securing six different objects, which included the settlement of all British-American differences, and the recognition of principles of international law for which the United States had contended for the past twenty-five years or more.[1] A day or so later, after King had revised and extended this list, it was referred by the Senate to the committee on foreign relations.[2]

[1] *Sen. Exec. Jour.*, III. 7.

[2] *Ibid.*, pp. 8–9. Negotiations were to be entered into for the purpose:

"1. Of opening and establishing, on a satisfactory footing, the navigation, trade, and intercourse between the United States, and His Majesty's colonies in the West Indies, and on the continent of America.

"2. Of re-opening to the United States the navigation of the river St. Lawrence, between their northern boundary and the city of Quebec; of obtaining to them the navigation of that river between Quebec and the ocean; and obtaining for the trade of the United States in that quarter, by the grant of a suitable equivalent, a place of deposit on either bank of the St. Lawrence, within the province of Lower Canada.

"3. Of abolishing the duties imposed on goods and merchandise, exported from His Majesty's European dominions to the United States, or of reserving to them a right to countervail the same, by other and adequate duties; and of placing the vessels of both parties on the same footing, in respect to the amount of drawbacks.

"4. Of agreeing on and establishing adequate stipulations for the protection of American seamen from British impressment.

"5. Of defining the cases which alone shall be deemed lawful blockades.

"6. Of enumerating the articles which alone shall be deemed contraband of war.

"7. Of providing suitable regulations for the prosecution of neutral trade, with the colonies of the enemy of either party.

"8. Of protecting the vessels and merchandise of each, from loss or damage by reason of the retaliatory decrees and orders of either against a third power."

Had Monroe been successful in securing the agreement of Great Britain to the eight objects in this revised list, international law probably would have been advanced at least a century, and Anglo-American diplomacy at once reduced to an exchange of complimentary communications and ornamental ambassadors. In reporting upon the resolution, the committee on foreign relations confined their inquiries to the considerations:

1. Whether there be any circumstances which call for the proposed advice; and
2. Whether there be not serious objections to the interference of the Senate in the direction of foreign relations.[1]

In relation to the first branch of the inquiry, it was the opinion of the committee that the executive had already exerted every possible effort to accomplish the purposes set forth in the resolution, and that the advice of the Senate would in no way aid his future exertions.[2] Upon this point the report states:

Is it probable that the proposed advice will aid his exertions? It can not be presumed that he entertains any doubt concerning the opinion of the Senate with respect to the interests comprised in the motion, and the committee do not perceive how the expression of solicitude on the part of the Senate in relation to the objects about which no difference of opinion exists can afford any aid whatever. Every nation in making contracts is supposed to consult its own interests; and it is believed the history of the world does not furnish an example of one party yielding its pretensions in consequence of the disclosure

[1] *Compilations of Reports, Sen. Com. For. Rels.*, VIII. 23–25.
[2] *Ibid.*

of unusual solicitude by the other party. Should, therefore, the proposed advice be adopted and made public, it does not appear that any beneficial effect would be produced; and if it be kept secret, as is usual in executive business (supposing it to be given by the Senate as a branch of the executive), it would be wholly nugatory.[1]

The report then takes up the second proposition, as follows:

2. The committee having endeavored to show that the resolution is unnecessary, they proceed to submit some positive objections to its adoption.

If it be true that the success of negotiations is greatly influenced by time and accidental circumstances, the importance to the negotiative authority of acquiring regular and secret intelligence can not be doubted. The Senate does not possess the means of acquiring such intelligence. It does not manage the correspondence with our ministers abroad nor with foreign ministers here. It must therefore, in general, be deficient in the information most essential to a correct decision.

The President is the constitutional representative of the United States with regard to foreign nations. He manages our concerns with foreign nations and must necessarily be most competent to determine when, how, and upon what subjects negotiation may be urged with the greatest prospect of success. For his conduct he is responsible to the Constitution. The committee consider this responsibility the surest pledge for the faithful discharge of his duty. They think the interference of the Senate in the direction of foreign negotiations calculated to diminish that responsibility and thereby to impair the best security for the national safety. The nature of transactions with foreign nations, moreover, requires caution and unity of design, and their success frequently depends on secrecy and dispatch. A division of opinion between the members of the Senate in debate

[1] *Compilation of Reports, Sen. Com. For. Rels:*, VIII. 24.

on propositions to advise the Executive, or between the Senate and Executive, could not fail to give the nation with whom we might be disposed to treat the most decided advantages. It may also be added that if any benefits be derived from the division of the legislature into two bodies, the more separate and distinct in practice the negotiating and treaty ratifying power are kept, the more safe the national interests.

The committee are therefore of the opinion that the resolution ought not to be adopted.[1]

During the nine weeks that it was before the Senate this report, the resolution, and the principle involved were thoroughly discussed.[2] Unfortunately the meager entries in the executive journal give slight indication of the nature of the debates. In the end, however, the Federalists refrained from pressing the matter to a vote, and upon motion of King it was ordered that consideration of the original motion and the report of the committee on foreign relations be postponed "till the first day of June next " — a non-existent legislative day.[3]

The able statement, made in this report, of the disadvantages inevitably attendant upon a regular and formal participation by the Senate in the negotiation of treaties cannot have failed to exercise a powerful influence in permanently establishing the principle which, in practice, had been acted upon for more than twenty years. Certainly since that time the Senate has only occasionally suggested to the President that certain negotiations be undertaken, or that certain definite provisions

[1] *Compilation of Reports, Sen. Com. For. Rels.,* VIII. 24–25.
[2] *Sen. Exec. Jour.,* III. 33, 37, 38, 40.   [3] *Ibid.,* p. 49.

be sought in negotiations originated by the executive.[1]

RATIFICATION OF THE TREATY OF 1816 WITH SWEDEN AND NORWAY

In connection with the discussion of Lord Harrowby's treatment of the proposal of the United States to ratify the King-Hawkesbury convention with the exception of the fifth article, it was stated that, for a long time, the American government frequently accompanied suggestions for such conditional ratification with explanations of those characteristics of our constitution which made them necessary.[2] No better example of this practice can be cited than that furnished by the negotiations between Sweden with reference to the Senate amendments to the treaty of 1816 with Sweden and Norway.[3] Inasmuch as the steps taken by the executive in the ratification of this treaty also illustrate the problems which may be imposed by the action of the Senate upon the President, the Secretary of

---

[1] Crandall, *Treaties, Their Making and Enforcement* (2d edition), pp. 73–74. Here are cited a number of instances in which such action has been taken. See also Lodge, "The Treaty-making Powers of the Senate," for an interesting discussion of the question. The occasions upon which the President has of his own accord asked for the formal advice of the Senate as a preliminary to undertaking a negotiation are fairly numerous. This, however, puts the matter on an entirely different footing from that of King's resolution.

[2] See p. 156 above.

[3] Very little has been published concerning this treaty. Lyman, *Diplomacy of the United States*, I. 453, note, simply mentions its conclusion and amendment. In Ch. XIII. Lyman gives an account of our diplomatic relations with Sweden down to 1828. The Treaty of 1816 was negotiated to replace the treaty of 1783.

State, and our diplomatic agents abroad, it is proposed to trace here the history of the treaty subsequent to its qualified acceptance by the Senate.[1]

The three articles rejected by the Senate gave the United States certain privileges in connection with the importation of West Indian goods into Sweden in American bottoms, and allowed Sweden compensating advantages in the trade between the Baltic nations and the United States.

The resolution of the Senate was passed in February, 1817,[2] not two weeks before Monroe was to succeed Madison as chief executive. The outgoing President evidently took no action towards ratifying the amended treaty, and it was one of the subjects which claimed the attention of the new administration. Apparently Monroe left Washington on his tour through the eastern and western states without having discussed the treaty with Richard Rush, temporarily in charge of the State Department. The matter was forced upon the attention of the department, however, by the

---

[1] Of the three articles rejected by the Senate, Article 3 provided that all goods, the growth, produce, or manufacture of the West Indies, which might be imported into Sweden and Norway in vessels of those states might also be imported in American vessels at a rate of duty not more than ten per cent greater than that paid by Swedish or Norwegian ships. Article 4 stipulated reciprocal terms with reference to cargoes originating in the countries surrounding the Baltic, and imported into the United States in Swedish or Norwegian bottoms. Mixed cargoes were especially provided for. Article 6 provided a means of determining what goods were to be considered as having been produced in the respective states. These articles appear in brackets in the treaty as printed in *Conventions and Treaties*, II. 1742, *et seq.*

[2] *Sen. Exec. Jour.*, III. 78.

necessity of formulating instructions for Jonathan Russell, who was in the United States on leave, and at this time was preparing to return to his post.[1]

In a letter written on June 25, Rush took the matter up with the President and discussed at length the courses of action that lay open to the executive. He stated:

The new treaty has been adopted with the exception of the third, fourth, and sixth articles. The two first relate to the West Indies and Baltic trade, and settle also the rule of paying duties on a mixed cargo. The sixth barely prescribes the evidence which is to stamp the reality of what purports to be the articles of the growth, produce or manufacture of each country respectively.

As to these three articles, the necessity for any speculative inquiry or opinion upon their nature or probable operation, is, I presume, at an end. The Senate has seen fit to reject them.

. . . .

The question then is, what do we expect, or what is it to our interest, or our intention, to ask?

Are we willing to take the treaty stripped of these three articles? Upon this head I need your opinion.

[1] On July 20 Rush wrote to Monroe saying that Russell had requested that his instructions be sent to Boston by the fifteenth, but evidently had not been there himself at that time. Rush wrote, "I hope that my letter of the 25th of June (I think that was the date) may place this subject before you with sufficient fullness to enable you to say a word to me, notwithstanding the din that surrounds you. If left to myself, I should simply instruct Mr. Russell to have the treaty adopted (should Sweden consent), with the mere exception of the three articles, making the proper explanation to that court touching their exclusion. But this is a step I cannot take without your sanction, never having heard the least opinion from you relative to the treaty." Rush to Monroe, July 20, 1807. Monroe Papers, Division of Manuscripts, Library of Congress, Vol. XVI.

If we are the instructions will come within the narrowest compass.

But will Sweden take it stripped of them? I cannot see why not, for to be frank, had they stood, it seems to me they would have been most to *our* advantage. Mr. Russell may be better able than any of us to answer the question.

If Sweden will not thus take it, does the whole treaty fall to the ground, or have we any modifications to propose, and what are they? [1]

The President's solution of the problem appears in the instructions which Rush drew up and forwarded to Russell under date of August 14. After referring to the rejection of the three articles, Rush proceeded:

The treaty being thus altered by the government, cannot longer be regarded as the same instrument which was assented to by the Government of Sweden. It is proper, therefore, that it should again be submitted to that Government with a view to its approbation in the shape which it now presents. In the event of its being approved, a new ratification, at Stockholm, will, of course, become necessary.

In apprizing the Government of Sweden of the exclusion by this Government of the articles in question after they had been regularly agreed to by a minister acting with full powers on its behalf, a task, will devolve upon you which The President feels a confidence will be performed with the best discretion and effect which such a case will allow. The true explanation must be sought in the principles and structure of the executive branch of our Government. You are well informed upon this subject, and will take care to impress the just views which belong to it upon the Court of Sweden. You will cause it to be distinctly understood, that it is a funda-

[1] Monroe Papers, Division of Manuscripts, Library of Congress, XVI.

mental law of our system, that every treaty made by a minister of the United States, with whatever exact adherence to his powers and instructions and whatever the nature of its provisions, is still liable, when presented to the Senate for ratification, to be modified, or even to be totally rejected. There are already precedents in our history of a similar exercise of this authority. It will be familiar to your recollection, that the Treaty of Amity, Commerce and Navigation between the United States and Great Britain, entered into at London on the 19th of November, 1794, and signed by the two Plenipotentiaries, Mr. Jay and Lord Grenville, had part of the 12th article relating to the West India Trade afterwards expunged by this Government, to which Great Britain subsequently assented. Of this precedent you will naturally make the fit use. Above, all, you will give the explicit assurance,[1] that the rejection of the articles must not be interpretated into the least absence of consideration or respect for the Government of Sweden. Any such inference, as it would be contrary to the fact would be painful to The President; and he cherishes the confident hope that it will not be drawn. On this head it is The President's particular desire, that your assurances should take a character of utmost conciliation, as truly conforming to the spirit by which alone this government is animated towards the Crown-Prince.

It may be, that Sweden will not accept the Treaty, diminished as it now is from its former state, under the mere repetition of the ceremony of ratification. In such an event it will be considered as null, and you are empowered to open the negotiation anew. In forming another Treaty, the instructions heretofore given you in the letter from the Department of May the 20th, 1816, will be your guide. It is not seen that any advantage would flow from this course. If pursued, it must lead, substantially, to the same result. Yet it will be at your

[1] Not unnaturally, the Senate amendments to the King-Hawkesbury convention were not mentioned.

option even to offer it in the first instance if you are led to think that it would be preferred by Sweden, and much more if there is reason to suppose that the other course would not be acceded to. It might thus prevent the dilemma of a refusal.[1]

These instructions are a revelation of the careful, tentative manner in which the United States in 1816 was attempting to adjust her diplomatic intercourse to the necessities of her constitution. The treaty not only had been signed by the Swedish plenipotentiary, but actually had been ratified by the King. The greatest care, therefore was to be taken to assure Sweden that the rejection of three of the articles which had been agreed upon did not imply any lack of respect for the Swedish government. Evidently it was thought entirely possible that Sweden would follow the example of Great Britain and decline to acquiesce in the amendment of the treaty. The instructions show clearly that the government felt that in the circumstances such action could not be justly resented by the United States, and authorize Russell to accept such a decision and to proceed with the negotiation of a new treaty. The suggestion that it might be inadvisable to request Sweden to accept the mutilated treaty is evidence that the American government realized that the proposal was not in accordance with the recognized practice of international intercourse.

Upon his return to Stockholm Russell at once proceeded to explain the situation to the Swedish

[1] Richard Rush to Jonathan Russell, August 14, 1817. MS. State Department, Bureau Index and Archives, U. S. Ministers, Instructions, VIII. 145, et seq.

government, and in December, 1817, he reported to the Secretary of State his first conversations with Count d'Engestrom, the Swedish minister of foreign affairs. These led him to believe that the treaty would "eventually be accepted with the retrenchment made by the Senate." [1] Early in January he submitted to Count d'Engestrom a written memoir which officially set forth the facts which he had been instructed to lay before the Swedish court.[2] After a brief correspondence upon the points at issue,[3] the Swedish minister decided that the changes made by the United States Senate were neither subversive to the interests of his government nor derogatory to its honor, and therefore, that the treaty might be accepted as amended. His formal notification to Russell of this decision sets forth the view of the Swedish government in the matter, as follows:

It is by the express order of the King, his August Sovereign, that the undersigned has now the honor to declare to Mr. Russell, that the three articles which the

[1] Russell to Adams, December 29, 1817, MS. State Department Bureau of Indexes and Archives, Stockholm Legation, J. Russell, 1812–1813, Vol. I.

[2] Russell to d'Engestrom, January 4, 1818, MS. State Department, Stockholm Legation, J. Russell, 1812–1813, Vol. I.

[3] Under date of January 22 Russell wrote to Adams, "In a conversation with Count d'Engestrom, on the 3d instant, at which Count Marnet, who also signed the treaty, was present, I was given very distinctly to understand that the treaty, as modified by the Senate, would be accepted by this Government. I was desired, however, to give a more formal shape to the explanations which I had offered on the subject that they might be duly submitted to the consideration of the Prince Royal and of the Council of State." Russell to d'Engestrom, January 22, 1818, *Ibid.* See also same to same, January 12, 1818, *Ibid.*

Senate of the United States has believed ought not to be adopted, being of no particular interest for Sweden, and having been proposed only in the belief that they would be agreeable to the American Government, the King does not place any importance in maintaining them. His Majesty accepts and ratifies, consequently, the treaty as it has been ratified by the Senate, that is to say, with the exclusion of Articles III, IV, and VI, and consequently he has ordered the undersigned to proceed to the exchange of ratifications to be carried out in the manner which you suggest, as soon as Mr. Russell shall have received the ratification of the United States duly signed by the authorities of that country.[1]

Russell agreed that the exchange of ratifications should take place at Stockholm,[2] and exchange was effected on September 25, 1818.[3]

[1] Count d'Engestrom to Russell, January 24, 1818, MS. State Department, Stockholm Legation, J. Russell, 1812–1813, Vol. I.

[2] The reasonable nature of this arrangement is recognized by the American negotiator in the following excerpt from a report to the State Department: "You will perceive that, as I suggested in my letter of the 29th ulto, the exchange of the ratifications is expected to take place here. I could not very strenuously object to this course after having been reminded that one ratification, duly executed by this Government had already been sent to Washington and returned hither without effect." Russell to Adams, January 26, 1818. *Ibid.*

[3] *Treaties and Conventions Between the United States and Other Powers*, II. 1742.

BIBLIOGRAPHY

BIBLIOGRAPHICAL AIDS

Channing, Hart, and Turner, *Guide to the Study and Reading of American History* (revised and augmented edition, Boston, 1912). Useful in solving bibliographical problems.

A. B. Hart, *Manual of American History, Diplomacy, and Government* (Cambridge, 1908). This manual is useful in the handling of secondary material, particularly on account of its references to specific topics.

J. N. Larned, editor, *The Literature of American History: a Bibliographical Guide* (Boston, 1902). "A bibliographical guide in which the scope, character, and comparative worth of books in selected lists are set forth in brief notes by critics of authority." This work is of greater usefulness in the evaluation than in the location of material. There is no separate treatment of any of the subjects directly under consideration.

J. B. Moore, *Digest of International Law* (Washington, 1906, 8 vols.) contains a multitude of suggestive references both to secondary and source material bearing upon many of the topics under consideration. It is an invaluable bibliographical aid in this field.

A. B. Hart, *The Foundations of American Foreign Policy* (New York, 1901). The concluding chapter, a "Brief Bibliography of American Diplomacy," so far as it goes, is useful in estimating the worth of secondary works. The arrangement is topical and each book cited is briefly described and weighed.

Justin Winsor, *Narrative and Critical History of America* (Boston, 1886–1889, 8 vols.). In Vol. VII, pp. 461–562, is given an estimate of earlier works on the wars of the United States, which is of value. Vol. VIII, pp. 413–478 is devoted to a description of the manuscript sources of American History, followed by a description of printed authorities, 1776–1850. The notes to Dr. Angell's article, The Diplomacy of the United States, Chapter VII, Vol. VII, are critical and suggestive.

J. S. Bassett, *The Federalist System.*

Edward Channing, *The Jeffersonian System*. (The American Nation: A History, Vols. XII and XIII, New York, 1906.) The critical essays on authorities which form the concluding chapters of these two works are useful in a study of any subject within the period covered.

Ben Perley Poore, *Descriptive Catalogue of the Government Publications of the United States, September 5, 1774–March 4, 1881* (Washington, 1885). Although practically superseded by more recent guides, Poore is still useful in the location of material to be found in the public documents. The work is in two parts, the first part being a descriptive catalogue chronologically arranged, and the second an index, alphabetically arranged.

Elfrida Everhart, *Handbook of United States Public Documents* (Minneapolis, 1910) is a well-arranged work which is of great assistance in mastering the mysteries of government publications. Part 1 deals with Congressional Documents, Part 2 with Departmental Publications, and Part 3 with Publications of the Independent Publishing Offices of the Government.

U. S., Superintendent of Documents, compiler, *Check List of United States Public Documents, 1789–1909*. (Washington, 1911. 3d Edition, revised and enlarged.) The arrangement is in accordance with a complicated, but uniform system based upon the organization of the government. This is the most valuable aid in finding documentary material; it is the key to the serial numbers.

T. H. McKee, compiler, (*Indexes to*) *The Reports of the Select and Special Committees, United States Senate* (Washington, 1887), barely touches the period treated in this study, as it commences with the year 1815.

Van Tyne and Leland, *Guide to the Archives of the Government of the United States in Washington* (Washington, 1907, revised edition by W. G. Leland) is a useful guide to the archives of the State Department and of the Senate.

A. C. McLaughlin, *Report on the Diplomatic Archives of the Department of State, 1789–1840* (Washington, 1906). This is an invaluable guide to the student who wishes to use the material in these archives. It estimates the proportion of material in the archives which has not been printed to that which has been; it describes and analyzes the various series of documents and the system of indexing for each one; it points out some of the difficulties in the use of the diplomatic correspondence that are bound to be encountered by the student who is not thoroughly familiar with the files of the department.

MANUSCRIPT SOURCES

In the Bureau of Rolls and Library are to be found the originals of the treaties of the United States. Each treaty is filed in a large manila envelope containing also the official statement of the action taken by the Senate with reference to the treaty. This is in the form of a transcript of the Senate resolution authenticated by the signature of the clerk of the Senate. Besides this document, which is missing in only a few cases, other interesting material throwing light on the negotiation of a treaty, its reception by the Department, its ratification, the exchange of ratifications, or some other phase of its history frequently has been filed. To each treaty is attached the ratification and the proclamation by the President, authenticated by the Great Seal of the United States and attested by the signature of the Secretary of State. The ratification precedes the treaty itself, and in case of amendment by the Senate the amendments usually are incorporated in the ratification rather than in the treaty. The proclamation is bound after the treaty. The treaties on file are divided into two series, the first comprising the perfected, and the second the unperfected instruments. Those in each group are arranged alphabetically by countries, and chronologically under each country. The perfected series are numbered from 1 to about 600; the unperfected from A to Z, and then from A1 to Z1, and so on.

The diplomatic correspondence of the United States is filed in the Bureau of Indexes and Archives. The reader is referred to A. C. McLaughlin's report on these archives for a description of this correspondence.[1] Most of the material bearing directly upon the subject in hand during the period under consideration seems to have been published, in one form or another. The principal value of this correspondence in studying the action of the Senate upon treaties lies in the fact that very frequently such action is explained by the Department in its instructions to the American envoy accredited to the other party to the treaty; or the possibilities of Senate action of a certain sort may be discussed; or the course generally followed by that body in given circumstances may be set forth. Frequently such information is unobtainable elsewhere. In addition, the effect of Senate action upon the government of the other party to the treaty may be most directly traced in this correspondence.

[1] McLaughlin, *Report on the Diplomatic Archives of the Department of State*, 1789–1840 (Washington, 1906).

For the early period the executive files of the Senate contain little
material that is not in print.   The file room is on the top floor of the
Senate wing and the records are filed in small steel cases placed in
a filing cabinet.   The documents are uncatalogued and unindexed.
Those pertaining to each session are folded into small compass,
tied with tape, and forced into the case in which they belong.   Apparently Congress has not seen fit to take adequate measures for
their preservation, or for rendering them available for use.   In
addition to material stored in the manner just described there are
numerous chests containing all manner of documents relating to
the executive business of the Senate, the condition of which is such
that its use would be a Herculean task.

The files of the Senate committee on Foreign Relations are
conspicuous by their almost total absence.   For the brief time that
the committee existed during the period under consideration there
are none at all, the student being compelled to resort to the official
reports of the committee, and the personal correspondence of its
members.   It is interesting to note, however, that until recently
the records of this great committee have received little or no attention from any one.   Until the time of Hawkins Taylor no official
record was kept of the meetings, although for the last twenty years
a brief journal of the proceedings has been preserved.   Much of
the most important business done by the committee, however, is
transacted by correspondence between the chairman and the Secretary of State.   From time immemorial each successive chairman
seems to have regarded this correspondence as being his own property, and has carried away such letters among the files of his personal
correspondence.   What has been left has been turned over to the
executive clerk, who has stored it with other documents in the
attic of the Capitol.   No attempt has been made to make this
material available for use, either by statesmen or by historical
investigators.[1]

[1] This information was derived from a personal examination of
such files as the committee possesses, and from conversations with
the late Senator Stone and Senators Shiveley, Smith, and McCum-
ber, of the Committee on Foreign Relations, with the clerk of the
committee, and with the executive clerk of the Senate.   Previously to December 20, 1794, the Senate sat with closed doors
in legislative as well as in executive session.   The result is that for
the years previous to that date the *Annals* contain no more than a
journal of the proceedings.   For the early sessions parts of records
of some executive sessions are included.   These are dangerous to

Public Documents

Journal of the Executive Proceedings of the Senate of the United States of America (Washington, 1828, 3 vols.). These three volumes cover the period from the commencement of the first, to the termination of the nineteenth Congress, — 1798 to 1829. They are journals only, and contain the record of the proceedings of the Senate in executive sessions and in a few confidential sessions. Vol. I covers the period from 1789 to 1805, Vol. II from 1805 to 1815, and Vol. III from 1815 to 1829.

Annals of the Congress of the United States (Washington, 1834–1856, 42 vols.). The period under consideration is covered by volumes 1 to 35. The several volumes are not numbered serially, but are identified by the name of the congress, sometimes of the session, and always by the period of time covered. Throughout the period the reports of the debates are incomplete and fragmentary. Many of the longer, set speeches were revised by their authors for publication, or if previously prepared were printed as written. But the day to day debates are far from being fully reproduced.

Walter Lowrie and Matthew St. Clair Clarke, editors, *American State Papers; Documents, Legislative and Executive, of the Congress of the United States; Class I, Foreign Relations* (Washington, 1832–1859. Folio, 6 vols., 1789–1828). In these volumes are printed the annual messages of the Presidents, their special messages upon foreign relations, and, so far as they were available, the correspondence and other papers on the subject submitted by them to Congress or to either house thereof; also many reports of Senate and House Committees, and miscellaneous documents. The documents are arranged chronologically as transmitted to congress, except the annual messages, which appear in a chronological series (for the period 1789–1815) in Volume I. It should be noted, that the documents which appear in this collection do not comprise all of the diplomatic correspondence for the period covered. Professor McLaughlin estimates that not more than one-fourth of the material in the archives of the Department of State has been printed here. And he adds, "The materials printed in the *State Papers* very often appear only in extract. It is unnecessary to say that, so far as their

use, however, as the account of the proceedings for any one day is apt to be incomplete, and in some cases no notice whatever is taken of executive business. In either case there is nothing to indicate the omission.

importance for diplomatic history is concerned, the omitted portions
are not the least interesting."

Lowrie and Clarke, editors, *American State Papers: Class II,
Indian Affairs.* In this series of volumes the same thing is done
for the documents illustrating the relations of the United States
with Indian tribes as is done in Class I for those pertaining to the
foreign relations of the nation during this period.

Hawkins Taylor, compiler, *Compilation of Reports of Committee on
Foreign Relations, United States Senate, 1789–1901* (Washington,
1901, 8 vols.) The subjects treated in the several volumes are
arranged as follows:

I. Claims of the United States against foreign governments.
II. The same.
III. The same; claims of United States citizens against the
United States; of citizens of foreign governments against
the United States; of consular and diplomatic officers of
the United States against the United States for reimburse-
ment and extra pay.
IV. Mediterranean Commerce; nominations; authorizations to
accept decorations; international exhibitions; miscel-
laneous matters.
V. Tariffs of the several countries; boundary and fishery dis-
putes.
VI. Diplomatic Relations with foreign nations; Hawaiian Islands.
VII. Diplomatic relations with foreign nations; affairs in Cuba.
VIII. Treaties and legislation respecting them; general index.

It is difficult for one who has been compelled to use this collection
to speak of it in terms marked by the restraint imposed by the
amenities of scholarship. Particularly for the early period, the
years previous to 1816, the work can only be referred to as a hodge-
podge of reports selected according to no apparent rules from the
Executive Journals, the Annals of Congress, and Congressional
documents, and arranged upon a system which can be intelligible
to no one but the compiler. Previous to 1816 no Senate standing
committee on foreign relations existed. Yet the compiler of this
work felt free to refer to any committee which made a report on a
subject which pertained to foreign relations as "the Committee on
Foreign Relations," without giving any indication that he was
speaking of a select committee which perhaps had an existence of
twenty-four hours only, and which never had been called "the
Committee on Foreign Relations" by any one but himself. Further,

while he selected for printing many of the committee reports upon matters concerning foreign relations, other reports he ignored entirely. And, finally, many of the reports which appear are unaccompanied by any citations to indicate the source from which they were taken, nor is there any general explanation which covers this point. On the whole, this ponderous collection has been rendered as nearly useless to the scholar as such an imposing mass of historical material well can be.

J. H. Haswell, compiler, *Treaties and Conventions Concluded Between the United States of America and Other Powers Since July 4, 1776. Containing notes, with references to negotiations preceding the several treaties, to the Executive, Legislative, or Judicial construction of them, and the causes of the abrogation of some of them; a chronological list of treaties; and an analytical index* (Washington, 1889).

The reader is referred to the preface of this volume for a description of previous editions of the treaties of the United States.

W. H. Malloy, compiler. *Treaties, Conventions, International Acts, Protocols and Agreements between the United States of America and Other Powers,* 1776–1909 (Washington, 1910. 2 vols. Sen. Ex. Doc., No. 357, 61st Congress, 2d Session). Also *Supplement* to above. Sen. Doc. 1063, 62d Congress, 3d Sess., Garfield Charles compiler (Washington, 1913).

This collection is better edited than is the Haswell edition but unfortunately Davis's notes do not appear in this edition.

J. D. Richardson. *A Compilation of the Messages and Papers of the Presidents,* 1789–1902 (Washington, 1905).

Senate Manual (Washington, 1918). In addition to the present standing rules and orders of the Senate, the manual includes *Jefferson's Manual,* and other useful material.

WRITINGS AND BIOGRAPHIES OF STATESMEN

With the exception of the Monroe manuscripts, in the Division of Manuscripts, Library of Congress, there is little, if any, unpublished material of this sort which bears upon the subject during the period under consideration. In the published correspondence, memoirs, and biographies of the statesmen concerned a considerable amount of information is to be gleaned. It is apparent, however, that these men were little interested in matters of procedure, or in recording facts concerning the development of institutions.

MONOGRAPHS AND SPECIAL STUDIES

S. B. Crandall, *Treaties, Their Making and Enforcement* (New York, 1904; 2d edition, Washington, 1916). This work originally appeared as No. 1, Vol. XXI, Columbia University, *Studies in History, Economics, and Public Law.* Part 1 deals with the treaties of the United States, Part 2 with those of foreign nations, while Part 3 is given over to a discussion of "The Operation of Treaties." The book is an historical treatment of the subject, and is based upon wide research in both published and unpublished sources, which are fully indicated in numerous footnotes. It contains a wide amount of information, presented in such form as to be readily accessible. The second edition is revised and considerably enlarged, and includes a digest of the decisions of American courts construing treaties.

C. H. Butler, *The Treaty-making Power of the United States* (New York, 1902, 2 vols.) is an extensive description and analysis of every phase of the treaty power of the nation. It is useful as a reference work, and in the footnotes presents a vast amount of material from the public documents, judicial decisions, the works of publicists, the papers and biographies of statesmen and jurists and from other sources. Chapter X (Vol. I) on the treaty-making power and the relations of both houses of Congress thereto, and Chapter XIII (Vol. II), on the treaty-making power as it has been exercised with Indian tribes are the parts of the work which bear most directly upon the subject of this monograph.

J. B. Moore, *Digest of International Law* (Washington, 1906, 8 vols.) is indispensable to the student of any phase of American history touching upon diplomacy or international law because it contains a very large amount of source material not elsewhere available outside of the archives in Washington, and brings together the best work of American and foreign authors upon the topics treated.

J. C. B. Davis, *Notes Upon the Foreign Treaties of the United States, Treaties and Conventions Concluded Between the United States of American and Other Powers since July 4, 1776* (J. H. Haswell, editor, Washington, 1889), pp. 1219–1406. "Davis's Notes" are familiar to all students of American diplomatic history.

Willis F. Johnson, *America's Foreign Relations* (New York, 1916, 2 vols.). Although deficient in its treatment of the revolutionary period, this book is, perhaps, the best and most complete exposition of the subject.

J. W. Foster, *A Century of American Diplomacy; Being a Brief Review of the Foreign. Relations of the United States 1776–1876* (Boston, 1900). A. B. Hart declares (Foundations of American Foreign Policy) that this is the strongest book on American diplomacy since the Civil War. It is useful in furnishing a general outline of diplomatic events.

J. W. Foster, *The Practice of Diplomacy: As Illustrated in the Foreign Relations of the United States* (Boston, 1906). This is a thorough work by a diplomat and a scholar. Chapter XII, concerning the negotiation and framing of treaties, and Chapter XIII, upon their ratification, bear directly upon the subject of this monograph.

Theodore Lyman, *The Diplomacy of the United States* (Boston, 1828, 2 vols.), although obviously antiquated, is still useful for the period covered (1778–1828). It contains considerable original material.

Eugene Schuyler, *American Diplomacy and the Furtherance of Commerce* (New York, 1886) contains little or no material bearing on the action of the Senate upon treaties, although it gives a fairly acceptable outline of many of the commercial treaties of the United States, and the manner of their negotiation.

W. H. Trescot, *The Diplomatic History of the Administrations of Washington and Adams* (Boston, 1857) contains some original material which throws light upon the action of the Senate on the Jay Treaty, and devotes rather more space than do most authors to the activities of the upper house. It is characterized by Bassett (The Federalist System) as "clear and fair, but not brilliant."

E. S. Corwin, *The President's Control of Foreign Relations* (Princeton, 1917). Chapter III of this work contains a discussion of the relations of the President and the Senate in the making, enforcement, and termination of treaties. It is not, however, exhaustive, from the historical standpoint.

E. S. Corwin, *National Supremacy. Treaty Power* vs. *State Power* (New York, 1913). Except that in the opening chapter the author discusses the general nature of the treaty-power as conceived of in the early days of the government, his work has little direct bearing upon the exercise by the Senate of this power between 1789 and 1817. With reference to the activities of the Senate during later periods it is of great importance.

Charles H. Burr, *The Treaty-making Power of the United States and the Methods of its Enforcement as Affecting the Police Powers of the States* (Proceedings of the American Philosophical Society,

Vol. LI, Philadelphia, 1912). "The Crowned Essay for which the Henry M. Phillips, Prize of two thousand dollars was awarded, on April 30, 1912, by the American Philosophical Society." As its title indicates, the general purpose of this essay is much the same as is that of Professor Corwin's. The introductory chapter, which includes an excellent sketch of the evolution of the treaty clause of the Constitution in the Federal Convention, will be found valuable in any study of the treaty-power.

Henry Cabot Lodge, "The Treaty-making Power of the Senate," in *A Fighting Frigate, and Other Essays and Addresses* (New York, 1902) is a stimulating essay, the purpose of which is to show that the Senate has the power to participate in the making of treaties at all stages, from negotiation to ratification, and that they have exercised this power upon a great many occasions from 1789 to 1902.

Gaillard Hunt, *The Department of State of the United States, Its History and Functions* (New Haven, 1914). This is an able work by an accomplished scholar who is particularly well qualified to write upon this subject by long service in the Department. The book is useful in many ways to those who study any activity with which the Department of State is connected.

INDEX